Paupers

PAUPERS:
the making of the new claiming class

Bill Jordan

Secretary, Newton Abbot
Claimants' Union

Routledge & Kegan Paul
London and Boston

First published 1973
by Routledge & Kegan Paul Ltd
Broadway House, 68-74 Carter Lane,
London EC4V 5EL and
9 Park Street,
Boston, Mass. 02108, U.S.A.
Printed in Great Britain
at the St. Ann's Press, Park Road, Altrincham
© William Jordan 1973

ISBN 0 7100 7547 2 (c)
ISBN 0 7100 7548 0 (p)

Contents

1 Speenhamland Come Back— All Is Forgiven

This book is about people who do not share in the prosperity of our advanced industrial state. Usually these people are given labels which act as convenient shorthand ways for the affluent to explain the existence of the poor; labels such as Unemployed, Disabled, Old Age Pensioner, Unsupported Mother, Ex-Prisoner. Recently other categories have been added to the list; Low Wage Earner, Large Family, Problem Family, Homeless Family. In some parts of the country the categories of Coloured Person, Foreigner or Catholic have similar implications.

The rediscovery of poverty came briefly as a shock to the many people who believed that it was one of the giants of the 1930s which had perished in the post-war era, when the Welfare State made us One Nation. However, the way in which it was reintroduced to the attention of the public by writers like Townsend and Abel-Smith has ensured that, for all its unpleasant connotations, it can very safely be discussed even in the nicest circles. Since 1965 there has been a stream of literature aimed at indicating 'gaps in the Welfare State'. The idea of a 'gap' reassuringly suggests that there is some sort of satisfactory overall coverage, but that it has holes in it which expose certain sections to hardship. It is based on the notion that a person's economic well-being can be understood purely in terms of the adequacy of one protective garment, the Welfare State, without reference to such factors as the economic climate or whether he has a roof over his head.

Poverty has come to be treated as a technical problem associated with the economics of growth. To deal with this problem, we have poverty specialists. Writers on social administration have assumed the role of white-coated assistants to those who run the economy, analysing, measuring, experimenting, doing their sums and recommending how they are to carry out their tasks of social engineering. The notion that poverty, like pollution, is a by-product of affluence which requires specialist treatment to neutralise its noxious effects is appealing for those who, like

Donnison see the development of the social services as 'largely brought about by those who work in the services' (D. Donnison *et al.*, *Social Policy and Administration*, Allen & Unwin, 1965, p.29). This gives rise to an approach which typically is 'concerned with income deprivation in a much narrower sense—a level of income sufficiently low to be generally regarded as creating hardship in terms of the community's prevailing living standard, and so requiring remedial action on the part of public social policy—in other words "poverty" which is sufficiently severe to be seen as a "social problem" (F. Lafitte, 'Income deprivation' in R. Holman *et al.*, '*Socially Deprived Families in Britain*, National Council of Social Service, 1970, p. 7). Only true poverty technician-specialists could end a study called *The Poor and the Poorest* as Townsend and Abel-Smith did, with the resounding anticlimax: 'Finally, we conclude that the evidence of substantial numbers of the population living below national assistance level, and also of substantial numbers seeming to be eligible for national assistance but not receiving it, calls for a radical review of the whole social security scheme' (Bell, 1965, p. 67).

The tools of the poverty technicians are poverty statistics. Every week, the columns of *New Society* are filled with their comments on the significance of the latest figures. But the study of poverty statistics tells us nothing about what poverty is doing to the poor, about how they think of themselves, of their better-off neighbours, of those who employ them or of those who govern them. 'The mere fact of differing income levels does not tell us in what sense those on the same level constitute groups or whether such groups can be thought of as constituting a "class structure" ' (J. Rex, *Key Problems in Sociological Theory*, Routledge & Kegan Paul, 1963, p. 28).

This is not another book of defining poverty, or mapping its extent. It is about people who are poor, and how this affects them. It is based on the idea that the economic factors which give rise to poverty have little to do with the Welfare State, and that piecemeal alterations to it can do little to change them. It is an attempt to examine the political and social significance of poverty, and to look at the underlying causes and effects of the drift towards a more unequal, more unjust, less compassionate, more turbulent and ultimately unviable society in this country. It is about the factors which bring economically disadvantaged people together, and what happens when they join together for collective action.

The political significance of poverty cannot be deduced from statistics. The way people understand their poverty depends on their conception of themselves in their society. The statistical approach to poverty may render its study more objective and neutral, but people make their own sense of being poor, and the interpretation they put on it determines the action they take about it. Very often interpretations of their poverty which give rise to the most dramatic reactions by the poor are nationalistic (as in countries under colonial rule) or racial (as in the United States) or religious (as in Northern Ireland). However, any interpretations which see poverty in terms of injustice and oppression may give rise to political action by the poor which is violent or revolutionary.

Politicians are not necessarily good at recognising such explosions in the making. Treating poverty as a technical problem can very readily obscure its deeper social and political significance. Writing in the 1950s, Anthony Crosland held up the United States for favourable comparison with our country as a society in which 'objectively, class differences are very much smaller' (*The Future of Socialism*, Cape, 1956, p. 249). Once such blindness has developed, remedies for poverty may be adopted which, although technically desirable, are socially and politically disastrous.

In this country, poverty has sometimes been a political issue, but the poor have not been a political force for over 150 years. This is something to do with the distinction which most English people unconsciously make between the deserving and the undeserving poor. Like the Charity Organisation Society in the nineteenth century, we tend to distinguish between situations in which the 'decent, thrifty working man' is suffering, and those in which he is not. During trade depressions like those of the 1880s and the 1930s, the poverty of these deserving cases has become a political issue, and seen as a fit subject for political action. In the winter of 1971–72 there began to reappear those familiar tracts— such as T. Gould and J. Kenyon's *Stories from the Dole Queue* (M. T. Smith, 1972)—which told us what decent, honest ordinary folk were currently having to endure. The corollary to this, of course, is that in different times it is perfectly acceptable that some others should endure exactly the same treatment, because they lack those same qualities. The poverty of the undeserving— of those whose destitution is long term, or permanent, and unrelated to the trade cycle—is treated as a social problem, to be dealt with by those same harsh authorities whose brutality scandalises the decent folk. Once the industrious and deserving are back in full-time work again, the political outcry dies down, and the rest are left to the workhouse, the charities, the local authorities, the social security officers or the social workers.

It has been possible to preserve this distinction between the long term social problem and the short term political problem of poverty mainly because the undeserving poor could be held to be poor through their unwillingness to work and to save. Any hard working thrifty person could, it was believed, escape from poverty. This is beginning to be recognisably no longer the case, and the technical remedies we are adopting for poverty—especially the introduction of selective benefits during a period of rapid inflation —are reinforcing the trend. What is politely called 'the poverty trap'—a combination of low wages, high prices and numerous rebates for the poor, which ensure that the harder they work, the worse off they are—is recreating a pauper class.

It is hard to imagine how a malevolent power might set about planning a disruption of the stable democratic system of this country more deliberately and more effectively than by bringing about this situation. It is recreating all the ingredients of the last period of acute political instability in our history, and bringing us much nearer to the political situation of such notoriously violent societies as the United States. In this way, the poor themselves, who have played no real part in politics since the Labourers' Revolt of 1830, may come, as in the USA, to occupy a significant political role.

Now that the dust is beginning to settle after all the fuss over the million unemployed, it is becoming clear that the present situation has very little to do with that in the 1930s. It is not a case of the decent British working man being denied the chance to do his honest day's work. Some decent British working men have been doing more than their share of work, including overtime, productivity bonus and piece rates, and have been doing quite well out of it, throughout all the fuss. We are left with many others who have not been doing so well, and who are unlikely ever to do well again.

Until fairly recently, it was widely assumed that the power of the Labour Party and the Trade Unions effectively safeguarded the interests of the whole working class, and was used as an instrument of achieving a more just and egalitarian social and economic system. This assumption was based on the achievements of the Labour movement in the immediate post-war period, which suggested that a full employment policy, based on the application of Keynesian economic principles, combined with progressive income tax and universal social insurance, was sufficient to enable the whole working class to achieve a steady improvement in its standard of living. The assumption has proved to be false. The gap between rich and poor widened in the 1960s, not because certain special categories of people were not covered by the provisions of the Welfare State, but because of structural features of our economic system, which were reinforced by government policies.

Technological progress and the consequent increase in the productivity of many workers have helped to create a situation in which the Labour movement is potentially split. Those workers who are employed in modern, technical, capital-intensive and science-based industries have the opportunity to produce a great deal more, and to be better paid for doing so. Those who work in old-fashioned, labour-intensive and less productive types of employment are denied the opportunity of increasing productivity. In many cases they are becoming redundant. For those who remain in employment, because their work is less important to the economy, its status is debased, and their wages fall further and further behind those of other workers.

The figures on low paid workers speak for themselves. Outside manufacturing industry, the lowest paid group in all the main categories of manual workers fell further behind the rest in the period from 1960 to 1968. The bottom 10 per cent earnings by men in the construction industry fell from 77 per cent of the average earnings for that industry in 1960 to 72 per cent in 1968. In road passenger transport, the bottom 10 per cent fell from 77 to 71 per cent of the average earnings: and in local government, the lowest group fell from 86 to 72 per cent. In the same period, men working in agriculture, which is the occupation with the lowest average earnings for men, gained a proportional rise in earnings which was substantially below the average for other industries (J. Hughes, in *Family Poverty*, Duckworth, 1971). In addition, the rise in retail prices during the period is very likely to have affected low paid workers more adversely than higher paid, making their relative position even worse.

A Labour movement that was truly concerned to maintain the standards of living of all its members and to ensure the solidarity of the working class would have taken steps to counteract this economic trend by its policies. Instead, the Wilson government, with the collusion of the Trade Unions, introduced the criterion of increases in productivity as the prime factor in wage negotiations from 1965 onwards. Workers in economically advantageous positions were thus given the opportunity of enhancing and reinforcing their advantages. Productivity deals in capital intensive industries achieved large pay rises. But for the other, disadvantaged workers, there was very little to be gained in productivity dealing. All they could do was to negotiate away their tea-breaks, and to bargain their workmates out of their jobs. They did. The so-called 'shake out of industry', the 'redeployment of labour' and the 'planned redundancies' were simply a means of bringing the whole weight of technological progress to bear on the workers in those industries which were least able to compete in modern conditions; of getting the union leaders in such industries to sell out the interests of their workers for the sake of a few extra shillings a week. The present unemployment figures are a direct result of government policy aimed against the security of employment of the most vulnerable members of the working class. Old-fashioned industries tended to employ older workers, who were already the lowest paid group. Over half the manual working men earning under £15 per week in 1968 were aged fifty and over (*Employment and Productivity Gazette*, 1969). Upon this group is now imposed the additional burden of highest unemployment rates (one-third of the million unemployed at the end of 1971 were over fifty). Labour government policies have left hundreds and thousands of middle-aged men in the areas with concentrations of old-fashioned industries with little prospect of ever working again.

The Labour government attempted to soften the blow of its policies directed against worse-off workers in several ways, particularly in its regional policies. The Conservative government abandoned regional policies, and in so doing has brought down upon itself much of the anger that its predecessors deserved. Its policies for increasing competition, its abandonment of 'lame ducks' and its cynical attitude towards unemployment were simply further developments of policies which were started in 1965. Furthermore, its social policies represent another reinforcement of the same trend, which divides low wage, disadvantaged workers off from their more productive counterparts, and develops a natural alliance between low-productivity workers and other non-productive groups like the unemployed, the disabled and the retired. The working class is being split into a high-productivity sector, represented by the trade unions, and a have-not sector, which must represent itself.

Those who analysed poverty in terms of gaps in the Welfare State provided the Conservatives with arguments for the fundamentally divisive social policies which they had been waiting to introduce. With magnificent disregard for the implications of their suggestion, Townsend and Abel-Smith concluded that 'part of the problem [of child poverty] could be dealt with at relatively low cost by allowing national assistance to be drawn despite the fact that the breadwinner is receiving full-time earnings.' They dismissed possible objections with the telling argument that 'assistance is paid to families receiving full-time earnings in several states in the United States and this policy enjoys the tacit support of the American trade unions (*The Poor and the Poorest*, p. 6).

Just as they willingly adopted productivity as a basis for their policy towards wages, so the Conservatives readily accepted this rationale for their social policies. They had long been arguing for 'selectivity' in the provision of benefits. Now they could use the pressure from people like the Child Poverty Action Group (CPAG) to 'fill gaps' and 'provide coverage' for children in families where the father was earning less than the Social Security rate as an excuse to take a momentous step. Following Abel-Smith and Townsend's suggestion almost to the letter, they introduced a measure which in years to come may well be seen as one of the turning points in British political history. The Family Income Supplement may appear, if taken as a measure of social administration, to be no more than a rather objectionable way of accomplishing a desirable end. Even though it is based on a means test, and has to be claimed in a stigmatising manner, it does provide some help to some low wage families, especially those with several children, an aim with which enormous numbers of liberal people had identified themselves since the CPAG was formed. The point about the Family Income Supplement, however, is that it does much more than this. By treating low wage earners as a social problem rather than tackling the economic problem of low wages, the government committed itself to a step which by the time of the next election will be virtually irrevocable, and which will eventually divide the working class into two separate categories, independent citizens and state paupers.

The 'relatively low cost' solution which had been so glibly advocated by Abel-Smith and Townsend on the grounds that it was acceptable in that haven of social and economic justice, the United States, was not a new one for this country either. At the time when the Family Income Supplement was being introduced, it was widely commented that it represented a return to the Speenhamland System. This was the notorious scheme for subsidising starvation wages out of the Poor Law funds which was adopted in 1795, and persisted until its abolition in 1834. This comparison was intended simply to attach a bad label to the Family Income Supplement, but the similarities between the two systems and the motivations of the two governments which introduced them are worthy of a deeper consideration.

The reasons why Tory governments adopted the same schemes at both times lie in the similarities between the two social and economic situations. The biggest common factor between the situations of 1795 and 1970 was the massive inflation of food prices. In 1795 the cause was Britain's war against Napoleon; high prices resulted from economic isolation in resistance to France's attempt to unite Europe. In 1970 the cause was Britain's determination to join the Common Market; the artificial rise in prices resulted from the decision to resist public opinion and unite with Europe. In both cases the dilemma for the ruling classes was the same. In 1795 the landowners were making large profits out of scarcity of food, but their labourers were in danger of starving. In 1970 the big-business class could see quick profits in European unity, but some of their workers could not afford to live on the wages they were paying them. In both cases, the rulers were threatened with public disturbances, or worse, if something was not done about the plight of the poor. In 1795 the revolutionary events in France and in 1970 the urban uprisings in the United States served as warnings of what might happen if no action was taken. In both cases, Tory governments adopted the same solution.

At both times the Tories were being encouraged by small and weak Liberal minorities to adopt the solution of a national minimum wage. Whitbread's Bill of 1797, which was never even put to the vote, was paralleled in the Liberal Party election manifesto of 1970. Sidney and Beatrice Webb's summary of the situation in 1795 applied equally well to that which faced the new government in 1970. 'The nation had a choice between regulating by law the conditions of employment . . . or subsidising the employers out of public funds so as to enable their industries to be carried on *as they were*, and yet permit their workers to live. In the Speenhamland Scale . . . the nation chose the second of those alternatives . . .' (*English Poor Law History*, part 1, Cass, 1927; 1963 ed., p. 423).

The merit of this system, from the point of view of the rulers was, in both cases, its tendency to make the poor more passive and submissive, and while saving them from starvation, to lower rather than to raise their expectations. As J. L. and Barbara Hammond said about the first Tory government to adopt the Speenhamland System:

> They were anxious that labourers should not get into the way of expecting a larger share in the profits of agriculture, and at the same time they wanted to make them contented . . . the Speenhamland System turned out from their point of view, a very admirable means to that end, for it provided a maintenance for the poor by a method which sapped their spirit and disarmed their independence. (*The Village Labourer*, 1911, Guild Books, 1948, vol. 1, p. 166)

Historians are generally agreed about the effects of the first Speenhamland System. 'The Poor Law which had once been the hospital now became the prison of the poor. Designed to relieve his necessities, it was now his bondage' (ibid.). The system of allowances to men in work kept wages down well below subsistence level. It created a vast pool of rural unemployment, and put most farm work on a casual basis. Many parishes adopted the 'Roundsman system'. 'The practice was for parishioners without employment to be assigned by the overseer to particular farmers who accepted in turn the obligation of providing work at such wages as they chose' (*English Poor Law History*, part 1, p. 190).

At Deddington during the seven winter months, about sixty men apply every morning to the Overseer for work or pay. He ranges them under a shed in a yard. If a farmer or any one else wants a man, he sends to the yard for one, and pays half the day's wages; the rest is paid by the parish. At the close of the day the unemployed are paid the wages of the day minus two pence. (*Report of the Royal Commission on the Poor Laws*, 1834, Appendix A)

Such systems took away all independence from the workers, and all dignity from their work. There are reports that the kinds of work given to Roundsmen included pulling carts, and other tasks usually performed by animals. Chadwick himself described it as 'practically a system of serfage or slave labour'. 'As his subsistence does not depend on his exertions he loses all that sweetens labour, its association with reward, and gets through his work, such as it is, with the reluctance of a slave' (ibid., p. 87).

The effects on the victims of the system are vividly described by contemporary writers. 'Instead of families of small farmers, with all their exertions, all their decency of dress and of manners, and all their scrupulousness as to character, we have families of paupers, with all the improvidence and recklessness belonging to a sentence of poverty for life' (Cobbett, *Political Register*, 17 March 1821). 'What is that defective being,' asked Gibbon Wakefield, 'with calfless legs and stooping shoulders, weak in body and mind, inert, pusillanimous and stupid, whose premature wrinkles and furtive glance tell of misery and degradation? That is an English peasant or pauper; for the two words are synonymous' (*Swing Unmasked*, 1831). He is 'listless and unsettled . . . needy yet pampered . . . ill fed, yet irritable and nervous, Oh! monstrous progeny of this unnatural system' (the Lord Chancellor during the debate on the Poor Law Amendment Act, 1834).

It is such a pauper class that the present government has again decided to create. Its determination to split off the poor from the rest of the population is made clear in the very different standards it applies to these 'lame duck' second-class subsidised citizens from the ones it holds out to its enterprising, competitive, independent and freedom-loving supporters. The latter are told that their excessive taxation will sap their initiative and take away the incentive to get ahead. What they need is the spur of competition, freedom of the market, the incentives of the rich prizes of success. For the pauper class the picture is very different. Poverty is nothing to be ashamed of; it is something to be declared over post office counters, at the Social Security office, in the doctor's surgery, at the Town Hall, by one's children at school, and everywhere where benefits are available to anyone who is willing to announce in public that he cannot earn enough to make ends meet. The fact that even these subsidies do not make paupers as well off in work as they would be if they were unemployed; the fact that all these subsidies have to be suddenly and disastrously forgone if the breadwinner of the family succeeds in attaining an income equal to what he would receive if he were unemployed; these facts are not recognised as disincentives to ambition and hard work. For the pauper, in the eyes of his rulers, is not the same kind of being as the free citizen; is not motivated by the same drives and ambitions; does not hope and struggle for better things. He is not in the same sense a human being at all. He is, in short, a pauper.

For the government, the creation of a special pauper class has certain advantages. It gives the appearance of dealing with poverty, but it also deals with it in a way which splits off those who might potentially be a source of radical demands for higher pay from workers who have a stake, through productivity deals, in the higher profits which will result from the new economic developments. Conservatives have never been able to resist the principle of Divide and Rule, which they followed in 1970 as they did in 1795.

This principle is, of course, in the long run a disastrous one, as is evidenced in almost every one of the world's most intractable problems from Belfast to the Middle East and Vietnam. This is never more vividly shown than where one sector of a divided working class is degraded to the status of paupers. Rulers suppose that paupers and slaves who are totally dependent must necessarily follow their economic interests and defer to their masters. They are deceived by the outward submissiveness which so often accompanies a desperate inner rage. They do not recognise that the pauper who seems willing passively to accept his dependence

P.—B

feels that he has nothing to lose, and can switch in an instant from sullen obedience to violent resistance.

One common manifestation of the resentment and desperation felt by paupers is a very high crime rate (such as those at present found in South Africa and the United States). Under the Speenhamland System, it was widely recognised that the vast increase in crime (which swelled the number of prisoners in one local gaol from 173 in 1807 to 573 in 1826) was closely related to the plight of the poor. 'In January 1829 there were 96 prisoners for trial in Bedford gaol, of whom 76 were able-bodied men, in the prime of life and, chiefly of general good character, who were driven to crime by sheer want . . .' (*The Times*, 18 December, 1830). Of these, eighteen were poachers, awaiting trial for the capital offence of using arms in self-defence when attacked by game-keepers; of these only one was not a parish pauper.

However, the same desperate resistance could take a more organised form. In 1816 the pauperised labourers of East Anglia revolted, rioting with banners demanding 'Bread or Blood'. Although no lives were lost, much property was destroyed, and several of the thousands of demonstrators were hanged. The Labourers' Revolt of 1830 was much more widespread, organised and determined. All over the south of England mobs took part in the burning of hayricks and of the threshing machines which were depriving them of employment. Two workhouses in Hampshire were also destroyed, and some mills and factories in Wiltshire. The insurrection shocked the government, and its leaders were harshly punished, two being executed and hundreds transported for life. It was noted that the counties where the rising was most strongly supported were precisely those where the Speenhamland System was most widely operated. In spite of the rise of trade unionism and growing political awareness of the working class in the towns, it was the rural paupers who alone expressed the revolutionary spirit of the times in organised, armed rebellion. It was not at Cato Street or Peterloo, but in the villages of Kent and Sussex that the last revolutionary attempt on English soil took place. It was 'the sudden revelation in 1830 of the danger of rural insurrection, with the continual extension of pauperism to the greater part of the agricultual population of Southern England, and even to the wage earners of some of the industrialised districts of the Midlands and the poorer parishes of the Metropolitan area' (S. and B. Webb, op. cit., p. 418) that brought about the abolition of the Speenhamland System, and its hasty replacement by the Poor Law of 1834, with its punitive workhouse test of need.

In order to deal with the political threat represented by the existence of a potentially revolutionary pauper class, the Royal Commission which discovered the extent of 'demoralisation' amongst the rural poor recommended that the labourer should be given back his independence, at a stroke, by depriving him of his allowances. The new Poor Law laid down that 'if the claimant does not comply with the terms on which relief is given [that is, he refuses the offer of the workhouse] he gets nothing; and if he does comply, this compliance proves . . . his destitution.' This principle of 'less eligibility'—aimed at making the situation of a person on parish relief worse than that of the poorest independent worker—was introduced in spite of the fact that, for many, real wages in 1834 were much lower than they had been in 1795 and indeed, as one Poor Law Inspector wrote in 1841, 'a family cannot be maintained in a state of independence out of the workhouse with the same comforts they have in it at a less cost than twenty-five shillings per week, and this is more than double the general agricultural weekly wages in England' (quoted in S.E. Finer, *The Life and Times of Sir Edwin Chadwick*, Methuen, 1952, pp. 83–4). The troubles and the hardships, the riots and the famines of the next twenty years were a direct result of the economic and social distortions caused by the Speenhamland System, a system that had been adopted, and has again been adopted, to protect the interests of the ruling class.

The parallels between the situation created by the Family Income Supplement and that of the Speenhamland System are fairly close. During the first year after the general election of 1970, prices rose by over 10 per cent and there is every reason to suppose that during the period leading up to full participation in the Common Market economy they will rise as fast or faster. This means that in the five years that the present government will be in office, prices will rise by 50 per cent. There is evidence from the experience of the last few years that the wages of some workers may rise by this much, but that those in low-productivity jobs and at the bottom of the scale are almost certain to drop further behind, and also to be most directly affected by the largest rises, which will be in food prices. As prices go up, the 'prescribed amount' of earnings which qualify a man for Family Income Supplement will have to be raised also (as has happened already). Since low wages will fail to keep up with these rises in the prescribed amount, the number of workers who qualify for Family Income Supplement will increase.

As in the early days of Speenhamland the 'take-up rate' of Family Income Supplement is at present very low. Few people know about it, and fewer are willing to undergo the stigmatising process of claiming it. But as prices rise, low wage earners will be forced to claim this and other state subsidies in order to survive, and once they do so, the process of pauperisation starts. An ever greater proportion of low wage earners will join the increasingly identifiable, and potentially demoralised sector of society which is diagnosed as constituting a 'social problem', but which is in fact the product of our social and economic system.

It might be thought that the proportion of the population which potentially falls within the sector qualifying for the selective social benefits which the present government is introducing is very much smaller than the proportion of the population which qualified for the relief under the Speenhamland System. This is not the case. The proportions are likely to be roughly the same if we compare figures for the 1820s with the situation it is reasonable to predict will occur in the next two or three years.

A rough comparison can be based on figures for the County of Devon, whose position in the country's economy has not changed very much in the 180 years since Speenhamland was introduced. Then, as now, it was a low wage area. A Lancashire man's wage for cotton spinning in 1795 was £1, compared with a farm worker's 7/6d to 9 shillings. Furthermore, industrial work then provided more lucrative opportunities for the employment of women and children than agricultural work. In 1801, when the price of wheat reached its highest peak, there were 200 paupers out of a population of 1,200 in the parish of Berry Pomeroy, a village near Totnes in south Devon. The number fell again when prices went down, but when a new peak price was reached in 1812 they rose higher again, and after the war, although prices fell slightly, the totals exceeded any of the war years. It appears that the workers of Berry Pomeroy were reluctant to claim supplements when prices first rose and the system was introduced, but subsequently after being forced to claim to avoid starvation, became inured to doing so. During the 1820s between 20 and 25 per cent of the population of the village were paupers, young and old, employed and unemployed, though only about 18 people, mainly the very elderly, were ever in the parish workhouse. Many of those who received supplements had a trade or skill, so pauperisation was not confined to labourers (research by Mrs R. Freeman, Torquay Grammar School for Girls).

In 1968 the earnings of the lowest paid quarter of the men working in the south-west region were about £17.50 per week (*Employment and Productivity Gazette*, 1969). During the period 1968–70, the earnings of all workers in the lowest paid group (£15–£17) rose by an average of about 13 per cent (J. Hughes, in *Family Poverty*). Given that wages in Devon are representative of the region as a whole, this suggests that the average earnings of the men in the lowest paid quarter had risen by 1970 to just under £20, which was then the prescribed amount for Family Income Supplement for families with two children. This means that in Devon all workers in this sector with two or more children would have qualified for Family Income Supplement that year. But if the rate of increase in their wages over the following two years is the same 13 per cent (it will probably be less) and if the rate of increase in prices is the same 20 per cent in the following two years (as seems quite likely), then by the end of 1974 the average wage in the lowest paid quarter of workers will be about £22.50, but the prescribed amount for families with two children should be £24.00. Thus by some time in 1975 all families with one or more children of workers in the lowest paid quarter will qualify for the Family Income Supplement, and an increasing number of workers with larger families in the other sections will qualify. Therefore excluding people over sixty-five, who obviously form a much larger proportion of the population today than they did in the 1820s, but including the 6 per cent unemployed and the other recipients of social security of working age, it would appear that the numbers qualifying for the two supplements then and now are roughly similar.

The same sorts of calculations have been made in relation to other forms of selective benefits. The *Mid-Devon Advertiser* on 22 October, 1971 reported: 'It is possible that one in five of Newton Abbot Urban Council's housing tenants will be paying no rent if the government's fair rents legislation comes into force next year. Another 20 per cent would pay only a nominal rent, according to the estimate of the council's treasurer, Mr C. A. Moseley, in a report to the housing committee this week.'

What these figures show is that in an area like Devon, the system of supplementing wages and subsidising the poor will once again cut deep into the community, and, as in the 1820s, strongly influence the patterns of life of the large section which will thus be divided off from the rest. It will take some time to have this effect because such communities are still relatively homogeneous, and many poor people will strongly resist the economic pressures to submit to the stigma of selective benefits and wage subsidisation. In the meanwhile there will be much hardship among those who do resist, especially the elderly, for inflation will eat away their incomes month by month. But the younger poor will soon accept subsidisation as a way of life. Already men applying for low paid jobs are being told (usually inaccurately) that if they accept them they will qualify for large Family Income Supplements, and they are treating the continuation of state assistance from unemployment into full-time work as something they can take for granted.

In the cities, wage subsidisation on the Speenhamland pattern will add a new dimension to existing divisions already deeply splitting the rich from the poor and the slums from the residential areas. For some, pauperisation may be only a temporary feature, associated with a trade fluctuation or the loss of a particular job, an illness or the age of their children. But for many, living in the worst areas with the worst facilities, the worst opportunities for their children and the highest crime rates, the status of pauper even when they are working and earning will finally confirm their position as second class citizens, and take away the hope of any improvement in their lot.

Ever since 1834 the notion that a working man's dignity and self respect can be measured in terms of his ability to hold a job, which will make him an independent free citizen, has been one of the essential elements in the socialisation of working class children. It is embodied in the culture and traditions of even the most deprived communities, and is oddly reflected even in the norms of such adolescent subcultures as the skinheads. It is an essential part of the mythology by which the illusion of a just and free society is preserved; the shared consensus of all classes that, whatever his occupation or status, any man can, by hard work, earn sufficient to support his family. Once the institutional bases for this notion are cut away, not just by high unemployment rates (for the myth was not destroyed by the experience of the thirties) but by the system of supplementing wages, and the casualisation of unskilled manual jobs, then there is very little left upon which such a person can rest any claim to dignity and self respect. In work or out of it, in sickness or health, in youth or old age, he is simply a state pauper, unable to earn enough to feed his family, dependent on subsidisation for his bare existence.

Middle-class children are brought up to believe that the Welfare State is benevolent and generous (often too generous) in meeting the needs of those who cannot provide for themselves out of their earnings. Working-class children whose parents have had contact with Welfare State agencies are more likely to learn about the other side of their functions. Their regulations ensure that the meanest employer, paying the worst wages for the filthiest jobs, is not kept short of a worker while there is one able-bodied unemployed man available. All the so-called 'rights' to benefit are matched by duties to accept the dictates and directions of the authorities as to the acceptance of work, however unpleasant and the Family Income Supplement strengthens the position of the mean employer, by subsidising his starvation wages. At the same time, the administration of the Welfare State services ensure that benefits are rationed, both by the complicated processes involved, and by making claims procedures unpleasant and humiliating. Low take-up rates are not the result of ignorance or false pride so much as a reluctance to undergo processes which are intentionally deterrent.

Thus the present situation involves a clear contradiction. On the one hand, the system still demands obedience to the work ethic, and insists that all available jobs should be filled. On the other hand, this same work can no longer sustain needs, which must increasingly be met out of stigmatising state benefit systems. Thus work is no longer the means to independence, but instead becomes forced labour of a most odious kind, coupled with continued dependence on the state; a system exactly like that of the 1820s. Once work no longer confers the benefits of an independent status, once the worker is actually worse off than his unemployed neighbour, then work becomes sheer slavery, and the authorities who enforce it as a condition of benefit become the slave-masters.

This situation can exist in a disguised form if inflation which reduces the value of real wages is accompanied by a period of high and stable employment. Men who remain in the same job for a long time may be unaware of how much better off they would be if they were unemployed, for they will not directly recognise the falling value of their wage. But once they are made redundant—as so many older low wage earners recently have been—their situation becomes so much clearer to them. A job which had been a routine, made more pleasant by the companionship of long-standing workmates, is lost. After a period of unemployment, the authorities seek to get the man back into work in some new, less pleasant environment, on wages which are well below his level of benefit. Obviously he will experience this, far from being a satisfactory substitute for his old employment, as a piece of arbitrary authoritarianism, resented and resisted. His 'workshyness' is his fight against the authorities, based on his claim of the right to do work of his choosing, which will give him an income which will support his family.

As the number of job vacancies increases after the winter of the million unemployed, this is precisely the situation which faces many people. Often the new jobs are quite different from the ones which they have lost—different skills (or lack of skills), different conditions, different wages. The Department of Employment has recently begun to play a more active role in 'guiding' people back into work. They are first persuaded that it is in their interests to accept an 'alternative classification', often outside the trade in which they are skilled. Then they are told that if they accept an inferior job, they will still be notified of any vacancies occurring in their trades (an entirely empty promise). Gradually they are 'guided' into jobs, sometimes very short term in nature, which may have disastrous effects on their entitlements to benefit when they become unemployed again.

If the jobs are low paid, they find they are on a wage stop; if they are seasonal, they discover that they have no entitlement to unemployment benefit at all. It is thus in the interests of unemployed people who understand their situation to resist reclassification and job 'guidance' with all their might. To provide adequately for their families, they have to avoid taking jobs offered them, and cling to their rights to be supported on unemployment and supplementary benefits.

Although the ethic of hard work and independence has already been abandoned by a small group of disaffected people, mainly in the younger age group, it still sustains the majority of the worst off members of our society. If such people are to be denied any basis on which they can feel some personal pride, and if their whole experience is to label them as second class citizens, then they face a choice. Either they must accept the stigmatised status of 'lame ducks', forced into menial and filthy jobs, dependent on the whims of social security officials and intrusive judgemental social workers, with all the demoralising consequences of having to make Welfare claims for the means of their very existence, or else they must join together to resist the stigma of second class citizenship, to try collectively to fight for their rights for a better life.

What they will have in common is their dependence on the state for maintenance; all will be claimants on the Welfare State. As consumers of the state's subsidies they are already coming together in one organisation, the Claimants' Union.

This link between them is not as tenuous as it sounds. There has always existed as part of the culture of the poorest sector of our society an attitude of shared hostility to the agency which inherited from the old Poor Law authorities the responsibility for dealing with destitution. There is a kind of folk memory of the nineteenth-century systems, onto which has been grafted the experiences of the thirties, and which is one of the social determinants of the solidarity which exists between members of this sector. A common detestation of what is still referred to as 'the Assistance' or even 'the Parish' is even yet one of the strongest links which bind people in poor neighbourhoods together in a network of informal co-operative social relationships.

It is not only politically and economically that the present government has split off and welded together this sector of the

working class. Its first choice of method of dealing with poverty
—by supplements obtained through the Department of Social
Security—brings claimants as a group or class together to face
an institution with which they traditionally have a relationship
of conflict. At an individual level and collectively there is an
attitude of suspicion and hostility between poor people and the
Department's officials, which has surived the post-war years in
which poverty was forgotten by the other classes. It was easier
for those who 'rediscovered' poverty to forget the odious implications of a means test or a system of selective benefits than it
was for the poor to change their attitudes in a period when they
were never far from the threat of destitution. The sociological
consequences of government policy will be an intensification
of what was already a latent conflict between this group and the
institution appointed to deal with it, and that in this struggle,
claimants will become increasingly organised for conflict rather
than, as was piously anticipated, co-operatively aware of the
benefits of the system, and willing to accept their role as passive
paupers. The government's apparent change of mind, which
seems likely to substitute tax adjustments for the FIS scheme,
comes too late to obscure from low wage earners how their
economic position identifies them with the rest of the pauper
class.

That it is in their interests to organise and fight cannot be
doubted by anyone who has seen the Claimants' Union in action.
The Social Security system is not only a very stigmatising one;
it is also extremely arbitrary. A great deal of discretion is allowed
to visiting officers over the payment of special grants and in the
determination of the right to benefit of certain categories of people,
such as unsupported mothers and itinerant workers. In the
short period since Claimants' Unions began to come into existence,
they have shown that poor people acting together in support of
each others' claims can win payments from the Social Security
which would be refused to individuals acting on their own behalf.
It is therefore in the short-term interests of all claimants to join
together in this Union, with its conflict orientation towards the
authorities appointed to deal with paupers.

But in the long term, in spite of the changes planned to take
place in the methods of treating the poverty of low wage earners,
the interests of all claimants even more urgently demand solidarity

and collective action. For what is the prospect that faces this growing army of paupers? What can they expect from the ruling class and their allies, the Trade Unions and the Labour Party, who have called a truce in their old hostilities, and agreed to share out the country's prosperity, albeit unevenly, between them, to the exclusion of the rest? What will happen when the two sides of industry discover that it is too expensive to keep an army of dependents and semi-employed menials; when the social problems of inequality and injustice generate the kind of lawlessness and violence that has already been manifested in the United States?

The historical answer seems to lie in the Poor Law of 1834. The Speenhamland System was brought to an end when it was decided that it was too politically explosive, too expensive for the ratepayers and too demoralising for the poor. The solution to the problem that the ruling class had created was to make the situation of the pauper less attractive than that of the lowest-paid independent worker. Speenhamland was replaced by a system which gave the poor a choice between the freedom and independence (often to starve) of a first-class citizen (still paid second-class wages) or the complete loss of freedom and civil rights associated with the workhouse. The twentieth-century workhouse may take some different form, but the same choice may well be presented to the paupers of the future.

The Department of Social Security has not entirely forgotten how to run total institutions for paupers. It still has Re-establishment Centres for the long-term unemployed, which function as part of its machinery for 'the control of voluntary unemployment'. Here claimants are forced to undertake routine work for several weeks to ensure that they are not losing the habits of industry, and to remind them of the Department's power to penalise them if they acquire the attitudes of the undeserving. But these are not the only institutions run by the Department. Near Newton Abbot in Devon there is a former military camp, surrounded by a wire fence. It is inhabited by refugees who came to this country from eastern Europe after the last war. They live in cubicles, in the huts (which they call 'barracks') and they eat communally. Up to five years ago there were families living there; the children —some of whom had spent fifteen years there—attended local schools, but many of their parents could hardly speak any English. Little effort was made to integrate the refugees into the local community, and the many who still remain behind the fence are all now old but just as alien. They are seen at jumble sales and in the market, and sometimes in the woods, gathering berries and fungi. They live in a separate world, cut off from the rest, and kept first by the National Assistance Board and now by Social Security. The 'less eligibility principle' worked; those that could left, those that could not stayed.

It is not necessary to put a fence around people, or to give them a life of meaningless drudgery, to create a situation in which the state of pauperism is 'less eligible'. Whole communities could readily be given the status of latter-day workhouses by following the line first taken by the present government in relation to firms asking for continuing state subsidisation. A division could be made between those areas of the country which are economically viable and those which are depressed and dependent. Thus an area where there is high unemployment, a preponderance of unskilled casual work, low wages and few modern productive factories might form a natural unit for such purposes. The inhabitants, most of whom would be paupers anyway, could be offered a choice between an even lower and less free status, or emigration to a profitable area.

In terms of planning policy, something akin to this is already happening; in County Durham, for instance, some mining villages where the local pits have closed are being allowed to decay. Villagers placed in 'class D' for planning purposes are not only starved of resources for new development, but even denied the services necessary for basic maintenance. They are being allowed to crumble away, and those who remain in them are forced to choose between moving away or tolerating the ruins and squalor about them.

The same kind of decision about certain areas could be made in social policy. This would be the logical final 'shake-out'. Those who obstinately cling to local ties, or who know full well that they lack the skill or temperament to make their way in the technological zones, will have to accept the status of unfree workers, whose tasks would perhaps resemble those of prisoners or mental hospital patients. Law and order would presumably be maintained by methods similar to those which are used in such institutions.

There are certain parts of the country where areas could easily fall into this pattern. Northern Ireland (a final solution to this intractable problem?) the north-east and Celtic fringes would be natural situations for Bantustan areas in an otherwise prosperous province of the United States of Europe. As in South Africa, the two utterly unalike economies could co-exist within the same state, with the civil rights of the inhabitants of the two regions contrasting as starkly as their levels of prosperity.

Should people who face this prospect sit around and wait for it to happen? Should the victims of this shake-out do nothing to anticipate the next?

The Claimants' Union is potentially a mass movement of paupers anticipating the workhouse.

A movement which starts amongst the social outcasts; the dropouts and misfits, the industrially maladjusted, the anti-authority and the way-out political; spreading to the angry and frustrated, the long term unemployed with no prospect of employment, the middle-aged rejects of industry and those who have been carelessly maimed or debilitated by it; spreading further to include the stigmatised poor, the low wage earners, the large families and the others whose forced labour brings them less than a living wage; finally reaching the rank and file workers, who realise they are being betrayed by their unions into the hands of employers who will sooner or later use them up and throw them on the scrapheap with the rest.

Instead of continuing to believe in the promises of a technological paradise with more for all, an age of leisure in which everybody will work less and earn more, ordinary people will come to recognise the reality of a growing proportion of deprived and oppressed people whose lot is getting worse. Instead of believing in the myth of the bountiful Welfare State which looks after all unfortunate people, they will recognise the bleak and authoritarian features of our agencies for social control, and see that forced labour and dependence are no substitutes for freedom and self-respect. They will realise that today's worker is tomorrow's pauper, and that the price of higher individual productivity and greater personal gain, in terms of the human misery and degradation of those who have no share, is too high. They will come to condemn a system in which prosperity comes only at the expense of an ever-larger have-not sector of society. They will support the Claimants' Union in its stand, based on the co-operative and collective action of members of this sector, against the system which exploits them.

2 The Newton Abbot Claimants' Union

For most people, Newton Abbot is a town near Torquay on the outskirts of which they are likely to get stuck in a traffic jam if they go on holiday to the south Devon coast. Apart from its nuisance value as a traffic bottleneck, its appearance to a traveller on the Exeter to Torquay road is unprepossessing. Its skyline is dominated by a power station whose proportions belie its economic significance. The once-important railway yards sprawl across the flat and marshy ground to the east of the town at the head of the Teign estuary. In summer its approaches are usually powdered with the white dust of the claymines which pockmark the countryside to the west, towards Dartmoor.

Yet to the many holidaymakers who visit Newton Abbot during the course of their fortnight on the Devon coastline, these industrial encrustations do not obscure its function as a shopping centre and a market town. On a wet Wednesday morning in August the traffic in the town centre chokes to a halt as thin-faced Midlanders in bright shirts and plastic mackintoshes funnel in from the coast, mingling with the big-boned ruddy-faced men in coarse tweeds and rubber boots who pour in from the rich agricultural hinterland. Steamed-up family saloons jostle with muddy Land-rovers and trailers in the one-way system round the market, and the bleating of sheep merges with the wails of city children unwillingly dragged on a holiday shopping spree.

For the shopkeepers and the auctioneers, the smallholders with stalls in the market and the managers of the chain stores in the High Street, this is the moment when they cash in and grow fat in preparation for the winter ahead. But for the industrial workers of Newton Abbot, the summer season brings no prosperity. In 1971 the unemployment rate fell from 8.5 per cent of the workforce in the late spring to just under 6 per cent in July; but the seasonal jobs that brought about this fall were mostly menial and poorly paid. Newton Abbot is, by Devon's standards, an industrial town, but its industries have fallen on hard times.

A post-war engineering factory which came to the area for its low wage rates and once employed over 2,000 people, has contracted its workforce to under 1,000. An old textile mill had closed down, and so has a large old-fashioned factory which made clay pipes. These closures threw out of work many men who had been with the firms all their working lives. At a time when the number of unemployed nationally was higher than at any moment since the war, Newton Abbot's unemployment rate stood at nearly three times the national average.

Historically, it was the railway that transformed what was little more than a village into a busy little town of 18,000 inhabitants, and which gave Newton Abbot both its architectural character and its structure as a community. Spacious parks and a few dignified Victorian dwellings break up the closely packed rows of brick terraces which cling together almost as tightly as the kinship and social networks they sustain. There is something very worthy and respectable about these little communities, whose roots go back over a hundred years, and provide security in what must have once seemed precarious perches on the town's steeply sloping terrain. But even this security is threatened, for the railway yards, employing some 400 men, are under threat of immediate closure under a national productivity and modernisation plan.

Further out from the town centre are the post-war estates, council and private, separated from the town by the asbestos and plasterboard wasteland of the new industrial estate. These communities reflect the social and economic uncertainties of the period in which they were established; the retirement bungalows, detached for privacy, yet pathetically huddled together in terror of the final lonely wait for a sun-tanned death, far from kith and kin; the semi-detached family homes for managers and salesmen in the aptly named 'light' industries, the potteries, the sweet factories and the packing stations; the council estate, where the workers buy big rusty cars out of their uncertain pay packets, and wives work to make up their earnings to a living wage.

In May 1971 there was a public meeting in Newton Abbot, called by the Urban District Council, to discuss unemployment. The chairman of the meeting was the managing director of the clay company; the speakers were the chairman of the Council and the chairman of its Trade Committee. They spoke of the Council's efforts to persuade the government to give development status for the area, which had hitherto failed. There were then a number of questions and short speeches from the floor, mainly by businessmen and trade unionists. The meeting ended with the formation of a development committee of councillors, businessmen and union officials to look into the question of attracting new industry to the town.

One unemployed man spoke at the meeting; he was not from Newton Abbot, and his speech was ruled out of order because it contained political remarks in a non-political meeting. Another speaker announced that a meeting would be held the following week to form a Claimants' Union in Newton Abbot.

During the previous winter, Claimants' Unions had mushroomed all over the country. These Unions had virtually no national federal structure, and no permanent headquarters or staff. They were debarred from affiliation to the Trades Union Congress, because they were for people who were not in work. Each Union was autonomous, but several features were common to all; a membership consisting of people who were claiming Social Security; a concern for the welfare of all such people; a determination by members to support each other's claims and to fight against evasion, false information and intimidation by social security officers; and an opposition in principle to the wage stop and means test. Several unions had begun to circulate literature providing information about injustices by the Social Security; about tactics by which Claimants' Unions could fight against these; about the provision of discretionary grants and how refusals could be successfully fought at appeals tribunals; and about collective action by such groups as unsupported mothers to protect themselves from intimidation.

The meeting to form a Claimants' Union in Newton Abbot was held at the Labour Rooms on a May evening. It was attended in about equal numbers by unemployed people, who had received leaflets at the Employment Exchange announcing the meeting, and members of political groups in the town, one of which had been largely instrumental in calling the meeting. There were also two pensioners who had been in the Unemployed Workers' movement in the thirties; and the Manager of the Social Security office, who identified himself half-way through the meeting, to the consternation of some of those present. The total attendance at the meeting was about twenty-five. Ken, who chaired the meeting, explained the origins and purposes of Claimants' Unions. Ken was an engineer aged thirty, married with two sons; president of the local Trades Council; unemployed. It was he who provided the impetus for the formation of the Union in Newton Abbot, and who subsequently became its chairman.

The beginnings of the Newton Abbot Claimants' Union were not particularly promising. It was discouraging, but not surprising, that more of the unemployed, who were the only group of claimants to be notified of the meeting, did not attend. At first, the notion of a Union for people out of work sounds contradictory and improbable to people in a dole queue. Whereas it is possible, as we subsequently discovered, to appeal in some neighbourhoods to a shared hostility to the Social Security system, and to give organisational expression to a group's conflict with it, the same is not true of the way people experience unemployment. Claiming social security is, for many, an acknowledged long-term situation from which there is little chance of escape. For unsupported mothers, the sick, disabled and pensioners, their status as claimants is a long-term one; but even where this is objectively true of people signing the unemployment register, it is seldom subjectively accepted. The stigma to being out of work persists, even in a situation of high unemployment, and the notion that some kind of escape is just around the corner is adopted as a defensive rationalisation, even where it is practically unrealistic. Among younger unemployed men we frequently encountered the statement that they were just about to get a job out of the area, or to emigrate, or go to sea, in the early months of our Union's recruiting drive. It was only when months later we were still seeing them signing on, and the union had some solid achievements behind it, that we suddenly began to win their active support and participation.

Among the older unemployed men, in their forties and fifties, who formed the largest section of those signing the register, the experience of unemployment was a different one. For such a person, after what had often been twenty, thirty or forty years of unbroken employment, sometimes with the same firm, the shock of redundancy was bitter and shattering. Their well-established pattern of life was ruined, and they had nothing to put in its place. They reacted by depression and withdrawal from social contacts. Deprived of their established role in the community, they were

P.—C

lost. They felt as if they had no identity, and behaved as if they hardly existed in others' eyes. They scarcely glanced at our leaflets and hurried on when we spoke to them.

There still remains a question as to why, when whole firms close, or a large factory reduces its payroll by half, relationships established at work do not continue in a period of unemployment, and provide a basis for solidarity and co-operation among unemployed people. The answer seems to lie in a number of factors. New housing estates and better communications have meant that people who work together no longer necessarily live in the same neighbourhood, but are scattered among the community at large. But perhaps even more important, even if neighbours are in the same position, is the way an unemployed man is treated by those who deal with his unemployment. He signs on at the Employment Exchange and is interviewed individually; however many others are out of work, the department is geared to treating his problem as an unemployed person, not to treating unemployment. As time passes, with the routine of signing on, of interviews, decreasing in number with each week and month, he is recognised and recognises himself as a passive and helpless being, with no existence in time and space, except at a certain time on a certain day as one of those lining up in the dole queue. He experiences his failure to find work as a personal failure; he is increasingly isolated from others, both in work and out of it, because there is no shared activity and his inactivity is of a kind which cannot be shared. He develops the identity of a 'dole addict' existing only for the moment when he signs and draws. This is the only identity that is confirmed and reaffirmed each week in the faceless processes of the Department of Employment.

He is shunned by those in work who think that because there are vacancies advertised in the newspapers, the whole problem of unemployment has been exaggerated. He is avoided by those who fear contamination, or who dread the possibility of being expected to give sympathy or financial help. He reads in the papers the pompous pronouncements of politicians, employers and union leaders, betraying on every word how little they know about what it feels like to be out of work. No wonder, when he hears of some new organisation that is supposed to be for him, he cannot imagine that any such organisation could exist.

In our ignorance, therefore, we had in Newton Abbot tackled

the sector of claimants which was in many ways least likely to respond to the call for a union to be formed. However, there was a reason why this choice had been made. In any small town with high unemployment rates there may be a number of politically active people who are genuinely outraged at the effects of the economic situation on people's lives. But for such people there is a feeling of helpless frustration. A high rate of unemployment should serve to reveal the most glaring shortcomings of the economic system which they are identified with either reforming or overthrowing. Yet it puts those who might most want to change the system in the weakest position, since it leaves the unemployed unorganised, and without any means of making their voices heard. Thus the town's political groups may discuss Marx or Marcuse, while the elected representatives of the people argue over the siting of a public lavatory, and the dole queue gets steadily longer. Among the rest of the community, everybody feels that they are doing their best, that it is something beyond their control, that there is nothing more they can do. But there is a background feeling of guilt and shame; by those in work that they are doing nothing for those who are out; by the unemployed that it is in some sense their fault that they are there. In the last resort, at the end of every public debate or private discussion, there is a shrug of the shoulders, a sigh of resignation, or an apologetic disclaimer of responsibility. The whole thing is too big for us. It's out of our hands. What can a little place like this do about it? It's up to the government to put it right. Of course, it's all because of. We're just cogs in the big machine. What's it —— going to be like when we join the Common Market?

The small and ill-assorted group who started the Newton Abbot Claimants' Union were determined to challenge these attitudes of mind, for a variety of motives; social, economic and political. In other areas, the impetus towards a Claimants' Union came mainly from dissatisfaction with the Social Security system; in Newton Abbot it came mainly from the mounting unemployment figures. We were able to agree immediately that the policy of the unemployed members of the Union should be to provide for themselves an opportunity for improving their economic situation, through which they could discover that there was some way in which they could assert some control over their own destiny and do something about their position. The Union's activities had to involve people who were out of work in collective action which they could produce some immediate economic advantage for themselves, and prove at once that there was something that they could achieve in spite of their disadvantages. It was no good the Union blaming its potential members for failing to participate in its activities. It had to show people that participation was worth while.

We began by thinking of ways in which claimants could get together to improve their standard of living without infringing their rights to Social Security and unemployment benefits. The ideas which were put forward were simple and obvious, yet we discussed them half-jokingly, partly believing they could never work. We talked about a collective allotment, where unemployed members of the Union could work together to grow vegetables for free distribution to everyone in the union. We talked about buying groceries in bulk, and selling them to members on a non-profit basis. These were not new ideas. They were the characteristic reactions of members of the working class during a period of dislocation, when they were displaced from their customary social and economic roles by technological change and innovation. A yearning for a return to the land, and an increase in collectivism and co-operation were both characteristic of the years between 1790 and 1830 when, according to E. P. Thompson, 'the people were subjected simultaneously to an intensification of . . . economic exploitation and of political oppression' and 'were forced into political and social apartheid' (*The Making of the English Working Class*, Penguin Books, 1968, p. 217). It was in this period (the late 1820s) that the Co-operative movement was born; it had been preceded by the movement towards Friendly Societies and the first Trade Unions. All were based upon the 'basic collective idea, and the institutions, manners, habits of thought, and intentions which proceed from this' (Raymond Williams, *Culture and Society*, Penguin Books, p. 314). Those who, through unemployment, sickness, disablement, old age or some other cause, were now being driven into a new situation of apartheid, and those whose interests these original working class organisations no longer served, were once again meeting together to plan co-operative schemes of self-help, starting with a return to the land.

These historical precedents were vaguely in our mind at these early meetings, but so were many questions about their present day practicability. Could such schemes be started and made to work again twenty-five years after the coming of the Welfare State? Was the gain from them so marginal that the effort would be too much? Would people accept the benefit from them, or would they confuse co-operative self-help with charity and turn away? As we talked, manic fantasy alternated with gloomy pessimism. Was this really better than nothing?

At the south-eastern corner of Newton Abbot, on the old road to Kingskerswell which still serves as a useful short cut for locals on summer Saturday mornings, there is a small square of brick terraces, fringed by newer bungalows. The area is improbably called Decoy, and visitors must think buses going there serve as some kind of misleading relief. It is mainly a railway community, and very stable. The houses come to an abrupt end just a few yards beyond the pub, and beyond them is a large area of allotments, sloping down from the road to a reed-choked stream. Beyond this is open countryside. From the top of the allotment field you can look right along the broad valley down to Torquay; to the left is the cooling tower of the power station and behind it the hills which roll down to the Teign estuary. On the opposite side of the valley is the private sector of the post-war building estate; behind are the Victorian villas of the established professional classes, spaced out on the south-facing slope of Wolborough hill, and ringed by noble evergreen and avenues of limes.

The allotments are run by the Co-operative Allotments Association, but the spirit of the members' activities is mainly independent, individualistic and competitive. Most of the allotment holders are retired, many of them railway men; their gardening wisdom goes deep, based on a lifetime of experience, and they are proud of their personal industry and its rewards. Not unnaturally, they tend to be suspicious of outsiders, and of new ways. Many of them can remember the thirties, and have little time for anybody who grumbles about present day conditions by comparison.

We had little idea that we were causing a major political crisis in the allotments committee when we asked if we could take over some of the waste ground in the far corner of the field. There was considerable urgency in our request, for by now it was mid-June, and already late in the year for sowing or planting crops that would be ready before the following spring. A hasty decision by some of the committee to let us have the land, which had been growing a luxuriant crop of every kind of weed for ten years, was later to be questioned by others who 'didn't hold with it one bit', and who felt they should have been consulted. But it was not only the lack of consultation that caused us to have adversaries amongst the allotment holders from the start. We were doubly suspect, because we were unemployed, and because we tilled our land together in a great big square, and not individually, in strips. There was much apprehension expressed about 'long-haired lay-abouts' and 'every Tom, Dick and Harry who would come and help himself', possibly to their produce as well as our own. It was argued that anyone who had a mind to grow his own vegetables could take on a piece of his own, so why have this big piece all together? When our first working parties arrived, the skyline was soon fluttering with a line of hostile watchers, who like the pigeons in the trees, kept up a distant but menacing communication about our activities. We were very glad of the support of a few good friends among the allotment holders, who eventually convinced most of the rest of our good intentions.

The piece of land we were alloted was in the corner of the field furthest from the town, at the bottom of the slope down to a stream. The ground was even, but bone-hard; the weeds a little less tall than on the adjoining uncultivated area because some contractors' vehicles had been running over it to dump loads of clay against the hedge in the bottom corner. It was because of this that the council had an agreement with the association to cultivate the land as soon as it was let, with the result that after a week of negotiations and pressure, and a stream of telephone calls stressing the urgency of the matter, a tractor was sent to spend part of one day clearing the ground and breaking up the surface of the soil.

The Union was thus the proud tenant of nearly an acre of dust and churned-up weeds, with nothing to put in it, very few people to work on it, and with almost as few to eat its produce, if there ever was any. However, the project had achieved a certain amount of publicity, for when we had made it known that there was to be a collective allotment on which unemployed people would grow vegetables for free distribution to all members of the union, the idea was mad enough to attract the attention of the local newspapers and television. A stream of suede-shoed reporters and cameramen relayed through the gate at the top of the field and picked their way down onto our dust-heap to find out for the public all about what we and the volunteer helpers we had attracted from local colleges and schools were trying to do to help the unemployed in Newton Abbot. Their reports, however distorted, produced the result we had hoped for. When Ken distributed more leaflets outside the Labour Exchange at the end of the following week, there were many people there talking about the Union. In two days he joined up fifty new members, and the following week ten union workers came to the allotment. Gradually, members replaced volunteer students as our workforce, and by the end of July the allotment was running on Union labour.

Meanwhile we had found a source of cheap winter greens plants, and the tiny shrivelled embryos of cabbage, brussels sprouts, broccoli, cauliflower and kale began to take their places, in rows of sixty, between the low walls of weeds and stones which we had laboriously raked off the surface. But as fast as we planted down the slope, these vestigial vegetables at the top became engulfed in a weedy backlash of docks, thistles, dandelions and couch grass. Hoeing became an even more urgent priority than planting.

July was an exceptionally hot and dry month that year in Newton Abbot. Only the night dew brought any relief to the pale and crinkled plants. At dawn the pigeons came out of the big tree in the hedgerow, and attacked the few tiny green shoots at their centres, or sportingly pulled up any that had not been firmly stamped into the ground. As the sun rose and the traffic began to buzz along the Torquay road on the other side of the valley, the last traces of cooling mist lifted from the intervening meadow and the railway line beyond. At 8 o'clock, up by the road at the top, the contractors' men started work. By a strange irony, they were preparing the site of a new council industrial estate, as yet unsolicited by prospective industrialists, and whose proposed rents exceeded any in the area, but upon which rested the authorities' scanty hopes for an improvement in the town's economic situation. The men working there were outside workers, imported by a contractor from an areas with lower unemployment rates to do the work of our local authority. By 9 o'clock the site was vibrating to the roar of their excavators and dumper trucks, as

the first of our Union workers began to file past them at the allotment gate to hoe and to scratch at the soil by our primitive pre-
capitalistic methods in their first tiny collective effort to build up
an alternative system.

It was these first members who transformed our allotment
scheme from the nice idea of a small and unrepresentative group
into a genuine Claimants' Union activity, based on the enthusiasm,
co-operation and collective effort of claimants working for claimants. There was Tommy, who had written from Torquay where
he was 'drowning in a sea of affluence' as soon as he saw the television programme; aged twenty-two, married, one son; he spent
his last few shillings on the bus fare to come to Newton Abbot
every week during the summer to work in the allotment. Bert, a
planning engineer, unemployed three months, having been made
redundant for the fourth time, after only recently moving to the
area with his wife and two children having sold up in the north.
Ron, aged fifty-five, unemployed for two years after being self-
employed for twenty years; married with grown-up children. Bob,
aged thirty-eight, still unemployed eight months after successfully completing an I.R.U. bookkeeping course; married with six
children. Jean, made redundant three months earlier from a job
in a drawing office; her husband also unemployed from the same
firm. Chris, married with a young baby, unable to get a job as a
draftsman on returning to his home area. Geoff and Albert, both
disabled, who had been working together in a factory which had
laid them off through shortage of work; both married with families. The only common factors for this group were unemployment
and disgust with the situation which brought it about for them.
They made the journey to this obscure and out-of-the-way plot
of ground on the outskirts of town to work on a project that few
people believed would produce any real results; because it represented the first stirrings of action by the victims of unemployment
against its consequences.

During July there were reports in the local paper of visitors
leaving the coast to go home half-way through their holiday
because they were overcome by the excessive heat on the beaches.
On our allotment the sun beat down equally fiercely on the
backs of our workers; the parched pink soil reflected its glare in
our eyes; the dust as we broke up surface lumps of baked white
clay dried our throats. But because we were together, the time

passed quickly; for many of us it was the first chance to share feelings about unemployment with others in the same position, and to talk of every possible solution, from emigration to revolution. In spite of the heat, and the slow progress dictated by our primitive methods, we began to feel a strange affection for our co-operative desert. Tommy was certainly describing his feelings rather than our gardening when he told a reporter, 'It's beautiful, man, just beautiful.'

In the evening, the planting continued; a line strung out to the hedge; the swing of a heavy mattock to rip holes in the stubborn ground; the stamp of heels to drive the plants home; the dusty tramp down to the stream; the bucket thrown out to the limit of its long string handle and sloshed up again between the reeds; the water seeping instantly down towards the roots; the four or five brave new rows, left for a last night of coolness before they faced the shrivelling sun the next day. By the end of July there were nearly three thousand winter greens plants, our investment for the cold months ahead; down by the stream, about three hundred lettuces, and some long rows of peas and dwarf beans. At last, in the first week in August, it rained. Our crops, which for six weeks had been struggling to survive, began to grow. We were ready for the next stage of our co-operative venture.

In a low-wage area, inflation may have more damaging effects on the poor than recession. In Newton Abbot, many of those redundant middle-aged workers in old-fashioned firms which closed down were earning wages which were little, if any, more than they could get in unemployment and social security benefits. The area has enjoyed few of the advantages of being part of an advanced industrial economy. Most workers do not benefit from the negotiating power of the big trade unions. Yet they share the high prices of the rest of the economy, and the high rents. A few years of rapid inflation unaccompanied by wage rises will be sufficient to pauperise a substantial part of the working population for the second time in two hundred years.

Newton Abbot is a shopkeepers' paradise. Only two of the big grocery chains have opened up stores in the town and even they, after a few weeks of price slashing, have tended to round their prices up to acceptable local level, which is well above that of the big cities. If times are sometimes lean in winter, there is always a bumper holiday trade for the shopkeepers to look forward to; and whatever the economic situation of the town's inhabitants, trade will still be good as long as the market serves an enormous rural hinterland, and villagers from as far afield as Dartmoor use the town as their weekend shopping centre. The shopkeeping interest has been well represented on the council, and in town which is notably short on facilities, especially for recreation and for young people, spending on the provision of car parks has been lavish. A £278,000 covered market and multistorey car park has recently been completed, while a private trust is being left to develop a recreational centre for the inhabitants.

At the public meeting on unemployment held in May 1971, one or two shopkeepers expressed concern about the problem. Therefore, when the Union decided to try to enable its members to buy food more cheaply, to help their social security money go further, we wanted to test the sincerity of this concern. As we expected, a letter to the Chamber of Trade suggesting a discount for Union members at their shops was flatly rejected. We therefore decided to reduce food prices to our members by starting a co-operative shop of our own.

The idea of poor people pooling their resources to buy in bulk on more favourable terms goes back to the beginnings of the co-operative movement. Like our own small schemes, the roots of this movement were in the notion of co-operation in more than the question of buying and selling. From the grandiose notions of Robert Owen there evolved the more modest and practical schemes of working people taking collective action in their mutual interest, and combining together, both as producers and consumers, to form a co-operative community. As in our scheme there were echoes of a return for the land. One of the original co-operative journals stated: 'The object of a Trading Association is briefly this: to furnish most of the articles of food in ordinary consumption to its members, and to accumulate a fund for the purpose of renting land for cultivation, and the formation thereon of a co-operative community' (*Common Sense*, 11 December 1830).

Sadly, this first movement did not live up to its ambitions, and although much of the same spirit was soon re-embodied in the more practical Rochdale model co-operatives, the present-day heirs to this tradition are more preoccupied with competition with their capitalist rivals. Although, as we were later to discover, the original principles of the movement have not been entirely forgotten, the attitude of the modern Co-op was well expressed to Tommy when, on enquiring about the aims of the co-operative movement at his local headquarters, was told, 'Sorry, you've got the wrong place. We just sell milk here.' Thus when we set out to establish the Newton Abbot Claimants' Union Food Club we felt that, far from duplicating the services of the local Co-op, we were providing a much-needed self-help scheme for those most vulnerable to price inflation.

Our aim was to find a supplier who would sell us foodstuffs at prices which were less than those in the shops. The Union's choice was the local Cash and Carry, and we made an open and public approach to the manager, explaining our scheme. The response was negative, and we were refused reasons. To us it seemed likely that local grocers had informed him that if he traded with us they would withdraw their trade. From this time onwards we became more devious, and we have kept our sources of supply a closely guarded secret.

Next we needed premises. A businessman in the town offered us an outbuilding to use for a shop, only to withdraw his offer later. But the Methodist Minister, Mr Tom Meadley, had always supported our cause, and the Trustees of his Church allowed us to use one of the rooms there free of charge, every Friday evening for one hour. Thus by the middle of August we were ready to make a small start with our co-operative Food Club.

By this time our membership had risen to over seventy, and included a small number of old age pensioners and unsupported mothers as well as the unemployed. The lettuces on our allotment were nearly ready, and they would be followed by beans and peas a week or so later. We decided that we would use the Food Club as a distribution point for the free vegetables as well as the discount-priced groceries. Now we had to let our members and our potential members know about the Food Club. We told the Press that on 20 August, a Friday, we were going to give away lettuces to our members outside the Labour Exchange.

Not all of us were equally enthusiastic about this plan, for which I must take the blame. It drew attention to our scheme, and it was a kind of protest, but it looked too much like a publicity gimmick that it partially was. The morning of the 20th was fine and bright and we picked the lettuces at 7.30 a.m. There had been much anxiety during the week. Would they be ready? Would they go to seed at the last minute? Bert, his wife Val, his daughter Jane and myself parked our car within sight of the Labour Exchange at 9.15 a.m., and saw a group of journalists, photographers and television cameramen waiting for us. We were able to plan our operation from where we stood, including what action we would take if the police arrived because we were causing an obstruction. But our biggest worry was about the reaction of our members and the others as they signed on.

Tommy joined us when we had taken up our position, and we distributed our leaflets pointing out that this was not a charitable handout, but the distribution of a Union benefit, co-operatively produced for claimants. We also drew attention to the shortcomings of the Welfare State, and to the fact that our lettuces were about the only benefits available to them which were free and not subject to a means test. But while all this was true, and our members knew it already through our meetings and the leaflets we had produced before, some were understandably reluctant to take a lettuce in front of the television cameras. In addition, of course, only a handful of our members were signing on at this early hour. The local reporters seized on all this, and hurried off to write that there was 'No rush for free vegetables at the Newton Abbot Employment Exchange.' One paper even quoted an unnamed man as saying, 'What we want is jobs, not all this charity.' The fact that we gave away five dozen lettuces to members in the course of two hours went unmentioned.

What we had succeeded in doing was to let our members know about the Food Club, details of which were given in our handouts that day and the following week; and potential members were told, more fairly in the television coverage than the newspapers, what we were trying to do. The following week we bought £8 worth of groceries out of our television fees; flour, powdered milk, dried fruit and other basic items that could be bought in bulk and repackaged. The prices we were able to set were about 25 per cent or more below those in the shops.

On the Friday evening we set up shop and waited. The meagre quantity of our purchases indicated our expectations. We thought that few members would come out specially in the evening to do their shopping. We wanted to try ourselves out, to see whether we could cope with the practicalities of running the shop. We were amazed when a constant stream of members arrived turning the church room into something very like a village store. Almost our entire stock was sold within the hour.

A month later, we changed the opening time to a Friday morning and extended it to an hour and a half. By then our weekly stock was worth over £25 and our range of commodities had increased and altered. We had started with very basic items, but we found that more exotic lines, if the reduction in price was sufficient, were equally popular. Our members enjoyed buying the occasional luxury and could allow themselves to do this provided they had the opportunity of a bargain price. Turkish delight, dates for Christmas, tinned fruit and chocolate biscuits took their place alongside the cocoa and caster sugar. What had started out in the shadow of the soup kitchen had come to be more like a delicatessen. Butter, margarine, sausages, tinned foods of all kinds, even Christmas wrapping paper were quickly snapped up. During the hour and a half every week, twenty to thirty families, pensioners, mothers with young children, fathers on their way home from the Labour Exchange and middle-aged couples came to do part of their week's shopping at prices which allowed them a bit more money to spend each week.

Like the allotment, the Food Club has stood the test of time. A year after these small beginnings it is still going strong, and we have never been short of volunteer staff, as Val and Bert gave way to Sid and June, who in time handed over to Fred and Kath. The atmosphere in the Food Club is friendly and relaxed, a village shop atmosphere, with city supermarket prices. Members can meet and talk; the Labour Exchange is just across the road; the free cabbages are readily accepted as our equivalent of Green Shield stamps; their feeling of belonging to an organisation that is doing something practical and useful: the co-operative ideal lives again.

The Newton Abbot Claimants' Union's zeal for co-operative projects for self-help in the first months after it came into existence was directly related to our concern about unemployment, and reflected a membership largely consisting of the unemployed. There were several motives behind these schemes, and several reasons why they were well supported by members. We were fed up with the waste of productive skills and energies caused by the unemployment rate, and these projects provided an opportunity for productive activity. They helped refute the notion that unemployed people were 'lazy' and 'scroungers', and they represented a kind of protest against a situation of enforced idleness and passivity.

However, also among the motivations for participating in our schemes were undoubtedly yearnings by many of our members for dignity and independence. In many ways, our projects were in that tradition of working-class collective action for mutual aid which rests on a determination at all costs to preserve pride and self-sufficiency even at a time of great economic adversity. This tradition, embodied in the early trade unions, friendly societies and co-operatives, goes back to the early years of the industrial revolution, since when 'in times of emergency, unemployment, strikes, sickness, childbirth, then it was the poor who helped every one his neighbour' (Thompson, op. cit., p. 462). It was interesting to discover later that the local Unemployed Workers' Union in the 1930s had initiated very similar self-help schemes to our own in Newton Abbot.

There were perhaps two main weaknesses in this tradition, from both of which we were protected by our increasing contacts with other Claimants' Unions through the National Federation of Claimants' Unions and through its literature. Nearly all the other Unions had been founded on a membership of people who were primarily claimants of social security; they had been recruited at the Social Security office rather than at the Employment Exchange. The fundamental difference of attitude lay in the question of claiming supplementary benefits.

Running through the tradition of working class mutual aid is a strong resistance to dependence on poor relief, which was greatly re-inforced by experiences after the 1834 Poor Law. 'Nearly all the distressed operatives whom I met North of Manchester . . . had a thorough horror of being forced onto parish relief,' wrote Cooke Taylor in the cotton depression of 1842. The same attitudes were carried over into the post-war period in relation to National Assistance and Social Security, and help to explain the reluctance of so many people, especially the elderly, to claim benefits to which they were entitled. However, this is not the only working-class tradition. There is another, just as old, which can be traced to the Irish labourers of the same period, the first years of the nineteenth century. Although these immigrant workers, who took on many of the hardest and dirtiest jobs to be done in the first period of industrial expansion, may to English eyes have 'lacked the Puritan virtues of thrift and sobriety as much as those of application and forethought', they brought with them a healthy lack of pride about making use of any sources of financial assistance available, and a 'good-humoured contempt of English Authority', coupled with 'an acute knowledge of legal procedure' (Thompson, op. cit., p. 476). They were willing to accept parish relief 'without the least sense of shame', and they even turned the notorious Laws of Settlement to their advantage, joy-riding up and down the country at parochial expense. It was this tradition to which the other Claimants' Unions were the rightful heirs, and whose inheritance they shared with us.

It was this tradition, rather than self-help and independence, which more obviously suited the situation of long-term recipients of social security, and those who had been pauperised by low wages. For people who can see no prospect of escape from the situation of dependence on state support, the notion of self-sufficiency through hard work—whether individual or collective—is fairly meaningless, and it was therefore to the recently unemployed that our self-help projects originally made their strongest appeal. It was only after some time that we began to appreciate this latent contradiction in our initial approach.

The other great weakness of the English self-help heritage was its excessive formalism. Not only could the Puritan ethic of independence lead in the direction of meanness and stuffiness; it could also tend towards a rule-bound legalistic structure. At the time when these organisations were founded, as Thompson has pointed out, 'the discipline essential for the safe-keeping of funds, the orderly conduct of meetings and the determination of disputed cases, involved an effort of self-rule as great as the new disciplines of work.' Unfortunately, the legacy of their administrative formalities is to be found in the hierarchical structure and the ponderously off-putting ritualism of modern trade unionism. Claimants' Unions rejected these impediments to direct democracy and sought a simple constitution in which members were encouraged to participate as equals, and assert genuine control over policy and decisions.

As a result, therefore, the constitution of the Newton Abbot Union, which was adopted in July 1971, was straightforward, and in line with those of other unions.

Objectives

1   To fight for, and to improve the interests of all Claimants and Unemployed Workers and to support all our members' claims without reservation.
2   The right to an adequate income, without means test, for all.
3   A completely free welfare state for all.

Constitution

1   The Union shall not affiliate to any other organisation other then a National Claimants' Union.
2   The Union shall appoint the following officers:
      Chairman
      Secretary/Treasurer
      Claims Secretary
      Publications Secretary
    to be elected yearly and by subject to recall at any monthly meeting.
3   The Union shall meet at monthly intervals, when all decisions shall be made.
4   The Union shall have two classes of membership.
      (1) FULL MEMBER (claimants) with vote; subscription 5p per month.
      (2) ASSOCIATE MEMBER (non-claimants) non voting; subscription 50p per half year paid in advance.

However, in Newton Abbot we continued to make the mistake of waiting for our unemployed members to raise difficulties with their Social Security claims, instead of making a direct bid to recruit people calling at the Social Security office, and to help them there. Because those claiming unemployment benefit were mainly the recently redundant, many were still unfamiliar with social security. The Union's claims function — providing information, advice and above all representation, especially over discretionary grants — had to be advertised quite extensively before it began to be used to any great extent. At first, we thought that the reason for this was the Social Security system was operating more efficiently and more humanely in our area then elsewhere. While there was probably some truth in this, we later found that the real reason was our own approach to the problem.

However, the successes we had with the few cases which members did bring to us served to advertise the union's claims functions, and the trickle of requests for help gradually became a stream. It was noticeable that although we had only a few members in Torquay (which is a separate Social Security area) they brought up many more problems with claims than our Newton Abbot members. In part this was a difference between the two offices; in part it was that we were attracting a different kind of member in Torquay; in part it was because Torquay is a different kind of community.

Torquay has a population of 53,000, and is a place of extremes. The community is deeply divided, and those who do not share in the holiday town's prosperity are bitterly resentful. The plush hotel belt and the luxury apartments along the front contrast starkly with the ingrained poverty of some of the drab concrete council estates to the north of the town. In winter, the families who cannot afford the bus fares into town recognise the millionaire builders and hotel owners who sweep past them in their Jaguars and their Bentleys as they trudge home in the chilly twilight. These were the men they spent the summer sweating for, only to be discarded for the winter. 'He waved to me,' said one member, 'And I waved back, and I thought to myself, "You bastard".' 'This is a hard place. When you're down here, they make sure they keep you down.'

One of our first members in Torquay was Cyril, father of a large family, who came to us with lots of problems with the Social Security. When we helped him sort these out, Cyril set about recruiting everybody else who was receiving social security on his housing estate, and the adjoining one, into the union. By personal contact, door-to-door visiting and detailed explanations, Cyril joined up nearly thirty members in less than a month. Meanwhile, Tommy had been working equally hard in the centre of the town, and from the membership that these two were able to create, a Torbay Union with a very different character from Newton Abbot's was born.

People in Torquay joined the Union because their experience

P.—D

of Social Security reinforced their experiences of an unjust social and economic system; because the way they were dealt with by social security officers reflected the way they were dealt with by their employers, by their local authority, by their Parliamentary representatives, and by their government. The Social Security officers who alternately evaded, misled, bullied, harassed or intimidated them had come to be the very embodiment of a system in which they felt they were trapped and condemned to a miserable existence from which there was no escape. Unlike the Newton Abbot Union, the Torbay Union was born in a spirit of bitterness, directed against the Social Security.

The Torbay Union, which came into existence in November 1971 when the membership in Torquay grew to such an extent that it could not possible be effectively contained in the Newton Abbot Union, was an alliance between two groups who had previously been mutually suspicious or even hostile. On the one hand there were the members from the council estates; local workers, redundant from the hotel or building trades, pensioners, unsupported mothers and disabled people. They had a strong loyalty to each other and to their estates, and were highly suspicious of outsiders. The other group of members were the flat-dwellers of the town; immigrants from the Midlands and the North, seasonal workers, gentler people mostly, with many different attitudes and ways of life, who had sometimes seen the others as hard, exclusive, intolerant and punitive towards them. They came together, not without difficulties, because they were united in their hatred of the Social Security.

October saw the winter redundancies and the start of claims for grants for necessary items of winter expenditure. Members joined at a time when they were applying for discretionary grants for clothes, footwear, bedding or winter heating allowance. They had come to expect a routine from previous years; a long delay, then a sudden intrusive visit, offensive questions, misleading statements and finally nothing. Others were in even worse straits; benefits refused, on the grounds that they had a better chance of employment in another part of the country. Many immigrants who knew the lack of accommodation and jobs in their home areas prefered to be unemployed in Torquay than to be unemployed and homeless in Birmingham or Liverpool. Such members joined the Union to fight for their rights against the Social Security.

We started by holding meetings in members' houses on the council estate. From the beginning they were better attended than the early meetings in Newton Abbot; in fact they were overcrowded, noisy, chaotic, disorderly, quarrelsome and very exhausting. However, they achieved two very important things before the official foundation of the Torbay Union. Firstly, they established the principle of claimants helping each other with their claims. Unlike Newton Abbot, where too much of the claims work was left to the secretary, Torbay members started by acting jointly in support of each other; by acompanying each other to the office, by making phone calls on each other's behalf, by witnessing visits and arguing each other's cases. The results were highly encouraging, and success bred greater confidence. The second principle was co-operation between the different groups and an active democratic approach to the work of the Union. In the early stages there were moves to make its organisation hierarchical and exclusive, to fine non-attenders, to exclude certain individuals, to exclude women, and to concentrate authority in a few hands. The Union survived these, adopted a democratic constitution when it was officially founded, and continued to grow and to attract support from both sources of membership. This has not been without mistakes being made; and there have been resignations as well as new members joining. Although the Torbay Union has the same constitution as the Newton Abbot Union, their approach to their work reflects the difference in their membership. In Tommy they have had a very diligent claims secretary, who has been prepared to work almost daily in the Social Security office, helping people with claims.

In Torquay, the union's activities have brought direct conflict with the Social Security, and have exposed some of the brutally repressive elements not only in that system, but in the way the whole community operates. The town's economy runs on cheap hotel labour; it is therefore a magnet for casual workers in the summer. The Social Security Department has evolved its own methods for dealing with these immigrants, aimed at ensuring that they are not tempted to avoid opportunities of unpleasant low-wage work. The union is engaged in a constant battle on behalf of people who have been arbitrarily refused benefit, or given one payment on arrival and told it would be their last. They have to fight against artificial restrictions on rent allowances. They are constantly combatting delays and inhumanities which spill over from the immigrant claimants to affect all the rest, including the sick and old age pensioners.

The Social Security system in this country operates in a state of tension between two views of poverty. On the one hand it is seen as a state of need, but on the other hand, our relief of it has never operated solely on the criterion of need. There have always been ways of distinguishing the deserving from the undeserving, and once destitution is seen as in any way resulting from a claimant's own wilful or negligent behaviour, he loses his right to relief. The distinction is clearly evident in the Ministry of Social Security Act of 1966. Section 13 says: 'Nothing . . . shall prevent the payment of benefit in an urgent case . . .'—an apparently overriding emphasis on the side of need. But Section 4(b) of the Second Schedule of the Act says: 'Where there are exceptional circumstances a supplementary allowance may be reduced below the amount calculated or may be withheld.' This is the Section which is so freely used in Torquay, and which can only be effectively combated by insistent reference to Section 13—immediate need through total destitution—by the claimant and his representative. In the light of the problem of proving that one is starving, which is the only immediate weapon a claimant can employ if he is refused benefit, it is easy to understand the Claimants' Union slogan: 'Bite the Hand that Feeds You.'

To represent claimants effectively in such cases requires persistence and courage in the face of evasion and intimidation. In the last resort, the claimant and his representative can only refuse to leave the office until they are paid. In Torquay, the department have on more than one occasion retaliated by calling the police, and in one such instance five Union members, including a pregnant woman and a mother with a baby in her arms, were forcibly ejected from the office with considerable violence.

Many of the Union's members in Torquay are struggling to exist on Social Security. They are fighting for the means of survival, and it is a day-to-day battle. Getting one's rights as a pauper can become a total preoccupation, leaving neither energy or interest for any other task. It is therefore no wonder that the Torquay union has developed no self-help projects, and taken no steps towards co-operative independence. They are engaged in an increasingly bitter struggle with the hated Social Security; a struggle whose violence is always in danger of escalating and spilling over into other areas of their lives, or on to the streets when paupers meet together in groups. At the time of writing, Tommy and six other people are on bail, facing a charge of riotous assembly after a violent confrontation with the police over the arrest of an eighteen-year-old girl for breach of the peace.

In Newton Abbot, a much more stable and less divided community, the violence and the bitterness of this struggle seem remote, even though people are conscious of the same forces affecting their lives. The Union has moved rather slowly into its work with claims, and has only gradually built up an adequate system of representation for claimants. At the end of our first summer an intensive leafleting campaign, aimed at drawing attention to discretionary allowances for winter needs, at last began to produce referrals of members' claims problems, while social workers who had heard about the Union's work also started to recommend clients with difficulties over claims to us. So we suddenly found ourselves very actively engaged in the field of claims, and as our reputation grew we were called in to act in cases in Plymouth and Exeter as well as Torquay and Newton Abbot.

The Union's tactics in dealing with the Social Security, which our members soon picked up and employed to good advantage, were borrowed from the literature we had been sent by our other Claimants' Unions. The first essential was always to insist on a written decision on every claim made. Only in this way could members make sure that they had an official decision, and were not simply being ignored or being made the object of the officer's whims or prejudices. The second rule was to appeal against every adverse decision, and for the Union to provide representation for every member who appealed.

Such representation was the one specialised aspect of the claims side of our work. Appeals tribunals are intimidatingly formal, and claimants who are inexperienced in dealing with such situations stand very little chance of arguing their cases effectively. The tribunals in our area were held in the enormous Council Chambers of the Torquay Town Hall, hardly the obvious choice for what is officially styled an informal hearing. It was clear to us from the start that such tribunals were quite unused to hearing a claimant argue his own case from a knowledge of the statutes or the regulations. Indeed, one of our representatives was criticised by one chairman of the Tribunal for being 'too legalistic'. The Commission's representatives of course invoke the Act and the Schedules to it, but the claimant is not expected to know about such things. We found that the kind of legal battle about the interpretation of the Act which we engaged in obviously threw the whole machinery of the process out of gear. Our cases took up more time and made procedings overrun their allotted period. However, our success rate was about 70 per cent, and we found ourselves representing an increasing proportion of applicants. By November, at one of the weekly sittings of the tribunal, we were involved in three out of six cases from Torquay, and two out of six from Newton Abbot.

These appeals reflected some of the more blatant examples of the inconsistencies and inhumanities of the Social Security system we were fighting. In one case, a man in his fifties had been kocked down by a car and sustained injuries which will disable him and may leave him unfit for work for life. He was advised to go to a solicitor to make a claim against the driver but, when he did so, he was informed that there was no case against the driver because of lack of evidence. He then received an £11 bill for the solicitor's costs in establishing this fact. Because he could not get Legal Aid to fight his case he had to pay this himself out of his Social Security money. When he asked for a grant to cover the bill, it was refused, although solicitor's fees are within the discretionary powers of the Commission. He appealed and won.

In another case, a man who had been unemployed for over a year discovered that he was being paid nearly £4 less than the scale rates for himself, his wife and five children under a wage stop. It took him six weeks to get the assessment from the Department which revealed this fact. When he appealed, the Department argued that the overtime he had earned in his previous job, which had made his normal wages higher than the scale rate, was not guaranteed overtime. In support of this argument they said that it could not have been guaranteed overtime or he would not have been made redundant. If it was not guaranteed it could not be taken into account. He won his case. After six months' fight he also got his arrears of benefit.

In a third case, a divorced woman who had been receiving maintenance for her two children from her husband until he died, and who had then successfully claimed a similar sum from the Social Security for the children, suddenly had these payments terminated without reason being given. After two months, when she had become considerably in debt, she received a decision that she would be allowed about a quarter of what she was given before. At the appeal tribunal, the officer argued that her earnings of just over £2 per week (which she had always had) must henceforth be taken into account in the assessment of the children's needs. She won her case.

We are now providing a more efficient, on the spot service to claimants of Social Security in Newton Abbot and we expect our claims work to continue to grow. We are aware that it is one of our most important functions. However, we see it as only one way of claimants coming together to work for their common good. It is just their first experience of the fact that if they unite together, they are not just second-class citizens, helplessly dependent on the bureaucracy of the Social Services. Once they become part of the collective action of the Union, they discover that there are ways in which people in such an apparently hopeless position can do something for themselves. Winning a claim or an appeal is just a first step; many members who came to us at their wits' end about their position with Social Security have discovered, once they could overcome this difficulty through the Union, a new strength and determination to carry on the fight against their whole intolerable situation. They have taken the initiative in recruiting others, or in participating in other Union activities aimed at breaking out of the stranglehold of social and economic misery which the system had put upon them.

One of the lessons which we in Newton Abbot have learnt from the Torbay Union is the efficacy of building up membership out of social contacts between claimants. Many long-term claimants of Social Security are known to each other, and the

Union can reach a great number of potential members through one person following up all his family and social connections. In this way, groups of claimants who already have a natural informal relationship between them can come together and work for the union. Instead of unorganised neighbourly hostility to the Social Security, they can share an active and planned campaign against its iniquities. This is the way we have increasingly worked, and built up a new membership of pensioners, disabled, sick and unsupported mothers, to balance the original unemployed sector. In this way we hope that both in our membership and in our methods we can balance the 'English' self-help and the 'Irish' claims maximisation traditions, and provide the best of both approaches for all.

What is more, as we always predicted from the start of our Union, it is not only those out of work who have recognised the value of an organisation to help people deal with their dependence on state subsidies. Many of our active members who have succeeded in getting jobs have continued membership because they are aware that, as claimants of Family Income Supplements or one of the other state benefits introduced by the present regime, they are still at the mercy of the same system, which no other union or organisation is fighting against, or capable of helping them to resist. Like the paupers in Torquay, they are identified with the class of claimants, rather than with those in work. As a final proof of their recognition of the place of the Union as a real challenge to the system of pauperisation which has been introduced, new members who have never been unemployed are joining the Union. They are doing so partly to ensure that they can get its support if they have to make claims for Family Income Supplements, rent rebates or the like, or if they become sick or unemployed. But mainly it is because they acknowledge and support the stand which the Union is taking against the process of pauperisation.

The effects of this process, and the attitude of mind of our members towards it, are well illustrated by the history of one of our members, Jim, aged twenty-eight. He has been disabled since 1962 as a result of an accident in which he fractured his hip. Because the accident did not occur in circumstances in which he could claim against his employers, he could not get any form of disablement benefit or pension. However, it reduced his earning power, and he has been forced to take low-paid jobs, and to endure several periods of unemployment. He has been out of work as much as in it during his ten years of married life. He now lives in a council house, and has two children, aged nine and seven. During the autumn he was made redundant from a job as a carriage cleaner on the railways. It was then that he first heard about the Union, though at first he was sceptical about its value. After some weeks of doubt, he joined, and since has become a very active and valuable member, who took over as chairman from Ken when he left the area.

In November, Jim was offered a job working for a local authority as a cleaner—a job which had been specially created for a disabled person. The pay was very low—£15 per week basic—but Jim was told that he could get 'up to £4' Family Income Supplement if he accepted it. He was keen to get back to work, so he took it. In fact, because of compulsory overtime at alternate weekends, his income took him just outside the limit for FIS, so he got nothing from this source. However, because he was forced to work such long hours, his injury was aggravated, and within a month he was totally incapacitated again. The employer was unwilling to make any concessions to him over his disability, so that when he recovered sufficiently to think of returning to work, he was faced with a most unpleasant decision. Either he had to continue to jeopardise his health by working longer hours than he should, or he had to give up the job.

He discussed the whole thing with his wife, and decided to give the employer an ultimatum. Either they must make some concession to help him, or he would leave. They refused, and he left. He was immediately suspended from unemployment benefit, but with the help of the Union, his case was accepted, and his benefit was reinstated.

Because of his disability, Jim is constantly vulnerable to pressure from the Department of Employment to accept miserably paid jobs, often under bad conditions. He is well acquainted with the authoritarian pressure that the Department can put on claimants. Because of this experience, he can help other claimants who, as frequently happens, are suspended from benefit when they lose jobs, or threatened with suspension if they do not accept low-paid work. He is also interested in helping old age pensioners and the sick and disabled with their claims. He now spends all his spare time on the work, having learnt its many aspects through the Union.

Jim's struggles to support his family since his accident has been a losing battle. It is harder and harder for him to find a job at all; it is now virtually impossible to get one which will provide him with the equivalent of his benefit for a basic week— the hours of work he can reasonably do for his health's sake. As he said to his wife when he decided to quit his job: 'We may as well face it, we're paupers, that's all. We've got to claim for this and that even when I'm in work, so what's the odds. I might just as well be on the dole, and do some work for the Claimants' Union. That way at least I can help some others, and you and the kids will be better off anyway.'

The self-help projects that we had started in Newton Abbot during our first summer had one important feature which made them unthreatening to the bureaucracies which administered state benefits. They were not strictly 'work'. They did not constitute 'gainful employment' for those who took part in them. They did not take the place of occupations for which claimants would normally be paid.

The fact is that a claimant's right to benefits under the Welfare State is entirely conditional upon his conformity to the demands of the economic system. A claimant who refuses to accept a particular job can be disqualified from both unemployment and Social Security benefits. In this sense, a claimant has no 'rights' at all, except in so far as he can establish that for some reason he cannot meet his needs within the work market. The Welfare State exists to meet people's needs which arise above and beyond those which they can satisfy for themselves out of their wages they have earned. But it must always serve the economic system first. It must make sure that its provisions do not become more attractive than those of the most unpleasant employment; and if some people find them so, it must harass and penalise them until they can be forced back into the labour market.

In the situation which prevailed in Newton Abbot, the contradictions and absurdities of this system were clear to our members. The available work was blatantly inadequate to supply every-day needs in an increasing number of ways. Wages were so low that they were having to be supplemented; rents and rates were to be subsidised. For a large proportion of the work force, inflation had meant that they could no longer earn a living wage. Particularly in this sector of low-wage employment, there were not enough jobs to support the workforce. Yet in spite of high unemployment, a man could still be refused benefit for leaving a job, or refusing to take a job, even if it was one in which he was required to work all the hours in the day for a wage which was insufficient to keep himself and his family. Filthy degrading jobs paying starvation wages were still pressed upon claimants on pain of losing their daily bread. Employers were free to impose punitive pay and conditions, in the certain knowledge that the Department of Employment could be relied upon to force unemployed men into the jobs they so generously were providing.

At the other end of the scale there were wastages and deprivations. Skilled or even professional men were being thrown out of work, especially by the large engineering firm in the town. Many of them had only recently been imported from other areas, brought there on pretence of a permanent position, and now with no prospect at all of a similar job in the neighbourhood. Even up-country there were thousands unemployed in their trades, and their chances were not much brighter. Big business had trained and rewarded them while it needed them; now it wastefully and inhumanly cast them away. Their skills, once so prized, were now worth nothing. For a few months they would be paid a higher dole, then they would be down to rock bottom with the rest. The process was inefficient and degrading.

It was the experience of these things that made our members question the whole business of work. Instead of being the means to self fulfilment, independence and the good things in life, it became something that was at best an activity controlled by a powerful few, which would be taken away at a moment's notice, and at worst, a form of forced labour that could arbitrarily be thrust upon a man on penalty of starvation. From the position of unemployment, the behaviour of those in work was far from edifying. Competing for overtime, making bargains to cram more work into every hour, they vied with each other for the right to toil harder and harder, for longer and longer. And for what? For the sake of bigger profits for their employers, who saw labour as a 'cost', and who saw technological progress as an opportunity of replacing men by machines. And this in turn was not an opportunity for better wages and better conditions so much as a threat to the security of employment of those who remained. Higher productivity meant saving labour costs rather than sharing the benefits of automated production among all. Workers were having to work harder to produce the means of their own redundancy and to concentrate more wealth and power in the hands of the few who could control their lives.

For unemployed members with skills, what was most galling about the system was its inefficiency, and the discrepancy between what they produced and the wages they received. For them, the chance to control their own work, to work for themselves in their own time, co-operating with their fellow-workers, and sharing in the decisions about production, would have cut out all the greed and the bungling of a top-heavy managerial system. For members with no special skills, the freedom to do the work they chose, and the reward of a living wage, was what they wanted. Neither group had any immediate prospect of getting what it required from the existing system.

What we began to think of was a way to make work the kind of thing we wanted it to be, instead of just waiting and hoping something like it would turn up. Our allotment scheme was a useful starting point. What it proved was that unemployed people could be productive once they realised that to be so they would have to initiate their own process of production. What we had in our allotment was a very primitive system for producing vegetables collectively, co-operatively, and under our own control. It worked, because those who worked there believed in it, and because the work done was for ourselves, not for someone else who was profiting by it. From this beginning we realise that we could produce things, by labour-intensive methods, because we were motivated by the desire to provide ourselves with useful work, and because we wanted to work together to build up something of our own. The disadvantages of the allotment were that our methods of production were so primitive and our products of so little value.

We realise that we needed more sophisticated methods to produce the kind of product that would have a market value sufficient to support us. What was more important was that most of our members were factory workers, not gardeners, so to engage them in our productive enterprise we would have to find a process which, though labour intensive, would result in a product in which they could take some pride. They would not be able to commit themselves to producing something ridiculously simple by some tediously repetitive process. Yet more sophisticated methods and products would require more expensive equipment to produce, and we had no money.

We refused to be daunted by these very considerable difficulties. One of our members, Chris, who had been a high-ranking army officer, and had held managerial positions in industry, was convinced that we could find ways of making work for ourselves through our own initiative and imagination. Others like Harry, a retired civil servant, and Sid who had run his own business, were equally enthusiastic. We had so many members with skills, but no one with money. Chris began to collect together members with ideas about providing themselves and others with jobs, but they all reached the same difficulty—shortage of money.

At the beginning of August an opportunity presented itself to the Union that was to give us the impetus to new thinking that finally took us over this hurdle. A new Community Association was in process of coming into existence in the Buckland and Milber areas of Newton Abbot. These were the new council and private estates, which a survey carried out earlier in the year had shown to be very short of community facilities compared with the rest of the town. The new association was pressing the Council to improve their provisions for the area, but it was also setting about raising money to build a community centre itself. It was suggested that the Union might help the association by constructing the necessary equipment for an 'It's a Knockout' contest, which could act as the main attraction at a Saturday afternoon fête, to be held on a playing field in the estate. In return for any voluntary work our members might do, the Association was willing to make the Union a donation out of the takings from the afternoon's entertainment.

The idea was approved by the Union, and a small team of members from the Buckland area began work on the site. We had, among other things, to build a swimming pool out of rough-cut planks from a saw mill, a task which demanded both the carpentry skill of Noah and the patience of Job. We were assisted by an army of local schoolchildren on holiday and thus incidentally provided a sort of holiday play centre for the neighbourhood. Our roughly constructed barriers and obstacles, together with the spectacularly eccentric wooden swimming pool, gave the site the appearance of a village green prepared for an orgy of medieval tortures, with the children joyfully preparing to torment the victims of our fiendish machines. Although the show itself was partially spoilt by bad weather, and certainly bore little relation to its television counterpart, we succeeded in doing our job, thanks especially to the hard work of John and Jock who had spent most of their week hammering nails and restraining over-enthusiastic juvenile carpenters. Their efforts were rewarded with a donation to the Union from the Association some weeks later, which we were able to distribute in gifts among members without infringing their rights to Social Security benefits. It was thus that, out of such an unlikely project, the idea for a much larger and more important scheme was evolved.

What we had come to realise was that, failing to raise the money to start a self-sufficient co-operative working unit of our own, there would still be ways of getting our members to work together for their mutual advantage, doing socially valuable work. There were many jobs which were for various reasons, beneath the notice of commercial firms, but which could quite appropriately be undertaken by the Union. If we could get the support of the public in doing useful work, we ought to be able to find a formula under which donations could be made to a fund from which our members could benefit in ways which did not infringe their rights to benefits. As long as we could establish that our members were *unemployed* within the meaning of the regulations, and as long as the gifts they received were not of items already covered by their Social Security payments, we could see no way in which we could be prevented from carrying out our scheme. Perhaps starting in this way we could develop independent co-operative units, including workshops for our skilled members.

During October and November the idea was discussed at Union meetings, and among a group of members who began to meet informally at the Drive Inn. By the end of November there were about thirty members who were enthusiastic to start the scheme, including welders, engineers, fitters, carpenters, painters, motor mechanics, landscape gardeners, teachers and labourers.

We tried to establish the legality of the scheme by making enquiries from the source of legal advice available to us, but this was difficult in view of the unprecedented nature of our scheme. We certainly realised that we would meet with opposition, and not only from the state bureaucracies.

First, there was the question of its effects on people in work. We realised that they might regard us as poaching their livelihoods. This was not our intention; we were simply aiming at a more equal and fair sharing out of work. A man in work could do as much overtime as he liked; he could work at weekends and do spare time jobs; he could even have more than one job at a time. But a man out of work was condemned to do nothing (if he did not want to end up worse off by having his dole money stopped) unless our scheme could succeed in enabling us to take our share of the work there was going.

The second question was connected with this one. It would obviously be open to objection if we used unemployed men to do jobs other than in their own trade. We realised that it would be unfair on those who had served apprenticeships in a trade if we were to use non-tradesmen for their type of work. However there were so many unemployed men in most trades that we could fairly readily provide workers for the majority of tasks. Thus after some debate we agreed in principle to restrict work to the trades we had available.

Third, we had to ensure that we did not undercut the rates of pay of men in work, thus possibly depressing wage levels. We decided that we would ask that donations in respect of work done should be equivalent to the going labour rate for the job. Even if we charged this, we would be very much cheaper than firms, since we had few overheads and made no profits.

The fourth point was the danger of further casualising employment in an already unstable situation. This was a real criticism of our scheme, but to us it seemed that the advantages of our plan out-weighed the dangers. After all, it gave us control over a situation in which we had previously been helpless. It provided members with an opportunity to cease to be victims of economic circumstances, and to start to be in control of their own destinies. It gave them the chance to experience something quite different from the economic system in which they had first functioned as cogs in a machine that produced profits for others, and then being discarded as unnecessary for their masters' purposes. It gave them the chance to feel part of their own system of production, under their own control, in which they made their own rules and worked in their own way; in which they could correct the radical faults they saw in a system of which they had been part. So we saw our scheme not so much as a further step towards the breakdown of the organised labour market and the disintegration of regular employment as a first step towards the creation of a new concept of employment, whose virtue was that it was irregular and disorganised, in the sense that it was neither regulated nor organised by the boss, but under the control of the workers themselves.

To us, our scheme seemed a necessary way of breaking into the vicious spiral of low wages and unemployment. As long as bosses could persuade men to work for wages insufficient to keep their families; as long as men would fight for overtime to make up their wages, rather than sharing work; as long as productivity deals swelled the ranks of the unemployed, there would be no improvement in the real living standards—the quality of life—of ordinary working people. We had to start somewhere in the process of getting people to see that they should be fighting for a decent income for all, instead of competing for the right to slave for a pittance. Once we could show that unemployed people could do work that was dignified and useful, co-operatively, sharing the benefits, and enhancing their real standard of living, we could expose the folly of collusion with a system which exploited workers so ruthlessly.

The cornerstone of that system was the regulations under which state benefits were provided or withheld. It was these regulations which gave the employer his power, for they allowed the authorities to force someone into a job, however rotten or badly paid it might be. It also allowed them to control the income that any individual could make for himself while receiving state benefits. This was the part which was so unjust. There was no limit to the low wages that an employer could pay; the state, through the Family Income Supplement system, had accepted responsibility for making up starvation wages. What it would not allow was for a claimant to supplement his state benefit in any significant way. Thus the state was willing to subsidise forced labour, but not willing to give claimants the right to work for themselves. We had to change this situation, to help our members resist pressure from the Department of Employment to take rotten jobs, and instead to give them the opportunity of doing really useful work, and of living a better life. If the claimants were really living better than those in work, then workers would want to share their work and leisure instead of striving for more overtime and making agreements that led to redundancies. Forced work for a boss would be less desirable, and the value of unalienated work, of doing one's own thing, under one's own control, for the sake of one's own and others' benefit, would be recognised.

At the November meeting of the Union, a small committee was elected to start the scheme; Barrie, in his twenties, married, his wife expecting their first baby; previously employed as a marine engineer and draughtsman; Jim, a staunch member of the Union since the early days; married with two children; disabled, but recently returned to work after a period of unemployment; Bob, his brother in law, married with two children, who had recently left the services; and Fred, in his fifties, a landscape gardener who had not worked for two years since contracting tuberculosis. The first task was to find headquarters for the scheme.

At first, the task proved most difficult and discouraging. An opportunity presented itself when a shop in the main street which was owned by the County Council became vacant for a short period at the end of a lease. The lessee was willing for us to use it until his lease expired, and it would have suited us well because of the very public position it occupied. But the chairman of the County Council committee who had the power to refuse permission for the whole arrangement was a local arch-Conservative, so this plan came to grief. However, some weeks earlier we had written to the district Co-operative Society asking if they would let us use a property of theirs that had become vacant and to our delight we received a letter to say that they were anxious to help. After brief negotiations we found ourselves in temporary possession of the Co-op Coal Office in the centre of the town.

The organisation of the scheme was an enormous task for our small committee to undertake. We had to offer, to a public we hoped would be sympathetic, the chance to give us work in the skills our members possessed. We would then have to give them an estimate of the labour rate for the job, which would be the appropriate amount of their donation to the Union. After this, we would need to get one of our members to the job, and provide him with the tools he needed to do it. Finally, we would have to devise and administer a system of distributing the money collected from our workers in a way which was seen to be fair and acceptable by them, and which did not infringe their rights to Social Security and unemployment benefits.

It was the last problem that occupied us most on the eve of the public launching of the scheme. We decided that we must aggregate all donations and deduct a proportion to cover overhead expenses (rates, heating and lighting of the premises, transport and clerical costs). Then we should make the rest of the fund available for all those who took part in the scheme, including those who were not doing work leading to donations. We anticipated that many who worked would not claim from the fund, but we placed a ceiling on the share available to any one member that was related to the hours he or she contributed, allowing those most in need to contribute more work. Claims were to be made for items not covered by Social Security benefits, and would thus be related to needs. At this stage we were as concerned with devising a scheme which could be seen to be equitable for our members than with the regulations which the Department could use against us.

We distributed leaflets at the Employment Exchange on the Thursday and Friday before the scheme was launched, calling members to come to a meeting on the following Monday morning. On the Monday, over twenty members attended, and several others had asked us to include them even though they couldn't get to the meeting. The members had plenty of questions about the scheme, but the atmosphere was enthusiastic and hopeful. Everyone welcomed the idea of establishing their own style of the right to work. There was no doubt that they felt this was the most important thing the Union had attempted and the response was accordingly greater. We had arranged for the office to be manned by members of the committee every day of the week, but in addition to the committee man we immediately found ourselves with volunteer typists and with a good number of participants who were willing to spend several hours in the week running errands or helping out. During the week many other members registered to take part in the scheme, and to increase the number of skills we could offer to the public.

The scheme's launching received coverage in the local press and on radio and television, and from the evening of the first day jobs began to come in. In the main they were very small household jobs of the kind that would have been beneath the notice of commercial firms; though there were also some larger jobs from sympathetic people who saw the value of what we were doing, and who were glad to have the opportunity of offering some help to the unemployed in a way which was acceptable to them.

However, the same publicity which brought us work and public support also provoked the opposition we had anticipated. On the Wednesday, the manager of the Employment Exchange telephoned us to say that he would suspend the unemployment benefit of anyone who declared that he was taking part in the scheme. It appeared that the small amount of national publicity the scheme had been given had called forth from the Department the sort of reaction that indicated its true function in the Welfare State. Its main job was to police the claimants of benefits to ensure that no one receiving state funds was doing anything that could possibly interfere with the labour market. Our members were supposed to be sitting, like cans of peas, waiting to be taken off the shelf by some employer looking for a bargain. Because we had dared to behave like human beings, and asserted our right to work on our terms, our behaviour was not to be tolerated.

But this was not the only source of opposition. The scheme was attacked in the Trades Council by a Trade Unionist who described it as 'blackleg labour'. One of our members who went out to give an estimate for a job was visited by Trade Union

P—E*

officials who threatened him with expulsion from his Union if he took part in the scheme. The member, who was in his sixties, was understandably intimidated, and decided to back out. Employers telephoned the television studios to complain about the scheme, and the newspapers which carried the story of its launching also included editorial comments to the effect that, though well intentioned, it was ill conceived and would result in an increase in unemployment. One even suggested that, if allowed to continue, it would 'bring the country to its knees'.

This opposition revealed yet again the extent of the hypocrisy of those organisations and interests which repeatedly bemoaned the unemployment rate. It showed once more that claimants as a group were condemned to a second-class status from which any escape was forbidden. Not one newspaper printed the argument, which we repeatedly stated, that we were trying to establish a right to work of our own kind for our members. The firms and unions who condemned our scheme approved the working of overtime by their workers; they condoned an employed man doing odd jobs for money in the evenings and weekends. But an unemployed man with no prospects of work for years ahead was denied the right to do anything in his skill or trade without jeopardising his security through the state benefits system. If he worked a single hour in the week, he lost a day's unemployment benefit, and his right to have his National Insurance stamp credited for that week. Thus he not only ended up worse off, but risked his future right to benefits and his pension. What we were trying to establish was a scheme under which we would work without damaging his interests, and through work could retain his skill as well as his dignity and self-respect.

We hastily held a meeting of the committee to decide what action to take in face of this threat to our scheme. We had told our members that we were convinced that it was within the regulations, and that by working under it they would not be jeopardising their rights to benefit. Now we had to let them know immediately that the scheme was being challenged by the Department of Employment, and that if they worked they might have their benefit suspended. At first we thought that we should encourage some, for instance single men who had less to lose, to start work in spite of this. It seemed worth it, to keep the scheme going. We had taken months to get the office and to build up our organisational capability. The work was coming in fast. It would be heart-breaking to see all our efforts waste away. But after much discussion we decided we could not let our members risk their basic security over the scheme. What we had built up once could be built up again. We had to settle the question of whether or not the scheme was within the regulations before we could go any further.

We made a snap decision that Barrie, the chairman of the committee, would be the guinea-pig who would provide the test case for the whole scheme. There were several reasons for the choice. He had been in on the planning stage from the start, so he knew exactly what was involved. Because his wife was expecting a baby, she was receiving a maternity allowance which provided part of their income, which could not be affected whatever happened. Even so, Barrie stood to lose £6 in unemployment benefit and over £4 in Social Security, and we had no idea how his future benefit would be affected. In this state of uncertainty, he went off to North Devon the following day to do a labouring job, while we contacted the Employment Exchange and told them that this was what was being done.

From this point onwards, our struggle was increasingly a legal one. When Barrie declared his work, he was immediately suspended from three days' benefit 'pending further investigations'. Two weeks later he was told that his benefit was disqualified on four grounds. He had, it was said, been following a gainful occupation; he had earned more than $33\frac{1}{2}$ pence per day; he was not available for employment on the days in question; and the work he did was not consistent with the full-time work for which he was classified. The decision revealed the harshness of the regulations, and of the way they were interpreted. We decided at once to appeal against the decision.

In February his case was heard before an appeal tribunal. We argued that he was not following a gainful occupation, any more than any other person doing voluntary fund-raising work for his voluntary association would be considered to be doing gainful work. He was helping to raise funds for the union. His work should be seen as sponsored work, similar to the activities of a sponsored walker, and the donation received by the union should be seen in this light, and not as pay. If this was accepted, it seemed to us absurd that unemployed people, including Barrie himself, should not be able to benefit from funds so assembled. Clearly unemployed people would be allowed to benefit from funds assembled from the sponsored work of people who were in work. Was it right that the unemployed should be allowed to receive charity, but not to raise funds for the relief of their own needs?

If we could establish the non-existence of gainful occupation, we had no need to prove the other requirements, on earnings, availability and consistency. In fact Barrie himself earned nothing, and was certainly more available for work than if he had not been doing the job, as he was on the telephone there. Furthermore, it was consistent with his full-time job, for he could have done it at the weekend if necessary. But all these points went against us, predictably, at the tribunal, and now we are appealing to the National Insurance Commissioner against the decision.

In the meanwhile, we continued the fight, confident that in the end we would find a way through the regulations. To expose the true nature of the restriction on claimants, we encouraged Bob, one of our committee, to do a day's work digging an old age pensioner's garden, under the sponsorship of the local meeting of the Society of Friends (Quakers). The Society agreed to sponsor the work, and to make a donation equivalent to the labour rate for the job to a fund for the relief of the disabled. Bob could not benefit from his good turn, because as an able-bodied man he could not possibly draw from the fund. We thought that this would put the Department in an embarrassing position. If they disqualified Bob, then they were in effect barring unemployed people from doing charitable work of all kinds. He would be equally barred from raising funds for Oxfam or the Save the Children Fund by such a ruling. But if they conceded the point in his case, then this opened the way to similar sponsored work which claimants could undertake for other claimants in categories other than their own.

However, the Department disqualified Bob as they had Barrie, and once again we lost the appeal. Following the grim logic of their first decision, they argued that the sponsorship of the Society of Friends was 'a promise to pay' and that the donation to the disabled must therefore be seen as his earnings.

In defiance of common sense and the normal meanings of words, the Tribunal ruled that this type of charitable gift, rather than being as we argued a conditional donation, was instead some kind of contract of employment. Bob's good turn cost him £3.25 in benefit, which has never been made up from any source; the Department's decision caused a local outcry. The case clarified just how determined the authorities were to break our schemes, and to put a stop to any resistance by claimants against their passive status.

If we had won Bob's case, we might have been able to start a small work scheme of a thoroughly altruistic nature, with able-bodied claimants working to benefit less fortunate people who were old, sick or disabled. As it is, this has had to be abandoned, and we are more determined than ever to beat the system, whatever the consequences. But the decision has been a setback, and has caused a shift of emphasis and a change of course within the union. Inevitably the short-term unemployed, the better qualified, the skilled and professional people, the ones most interested in the notion of an independent co-operative workshop, have tended to drift away from the Union, and we are left with mainly long-term claimants, concerned with supplementing state support rather than providing an alternative full-time employment. Our new plan is based solely on this notion, and makes use of the experience gained from Barrie's and Bob's appeal. From October, when the permitted earnings of an unemployed person go up to 75p per day, we will provide a couple of hour's work for members every day, enabling them legitimately to earn £4.50 per week. This in turn will be pooled and distributed as under our old plan, to avoid penalisation under social security regulations.

In the last analysis, our original work scheme was based on a miscalculation. We thought that, in a situation of high national unemployment, it would be morally and politically impossible to stop us. We underestimated the authorities' ruthlessness, and their political short-sightedness. Their reaction in this instance was typical of their policy of divide and rule. In the work scheme, we temporarily united the short-term unemployed, whose identification was still with those in work, and the hard core of long-term claimants. However, the authorities were determined to split these two, and as a result have created in our area a larger and more ruthless pauper group, with greater identification of their separate interests. As the others have drifted back to work, we are left in bitterness to work out our alternative way of achieving our ends.

One of the absurdities of the official line against our scheme is that, in its efforts to preserve the motivation to work of the short-term unemployed, it is further undermining the motivations of the pauperised hard core. A work scheme such as ours might incidentally have rekindled an interest in work among many people who had long since decided that it was to their advantage to avoid it, while it would have been unlikely to have taken away the desire for full-time employment of those whose earning power was well above their benefit level. The interaction between the two groups might have served to re-integrate some paupers into the working class. The authorities have made sure that no such change occurs, and instead have confirmed the long-term claimants' hostility towards work and officialdom.

But it is not only the Department that has shown up badly in claimants' eyes during this battle. The fact is that the reaction of all the established interests to our attempt to establish our right to work seemed to confirm more than ever that claimants form a class apart, which must look after itself. We have been condemned and put down by employers and trade unions alike, and by the state bureaucracies which served them both. We have been supported only by individuals and a handful of groups, mainly religious. Originally, we felt we should try not to antagonise the Labour movement, or to upset people in work. Now we realise that we will make no changes unless we are prepared to do this.

This is the message which is being communicated throughout the Claimants' Union movement, based in experiences like ours. In the words of a pamphlet distributed by a Staffordshire Claimants' Union: 'Claimants are not part of the Labour Movement. They have their own specific oppressions. The Claimants' Union is a movement of the "Scum". Do not work to change this life of employment, employ yourself to change life! There is no place for the unemployed within the system. Together with the emerging groups in similar struggles, we must *smash* it.'

The Newton Abbot Claimants' Union was started by a small group of people in a stumbling, groping way. It has grown in strength not only because it now has two hundred members, but because it has become clear that these members recognise their situation in society and the need to take the kind of action that the Union's existence and activities represent. The union's principles have become clearer as we have worked together.

Since the Newton Abbot Union was formed, we have gone some way towards establishing a whole set of alternative social and economic institutions for our members. People who have been forced to accept the status of second-class members of the community because they are dependent on state benefits have worked together, voluntarily to grow their own food, to provide their own retail services, and to set up their own system of work.

One of the difficulties we have faced is in overcoming the fatalism and inertia which is an inevitable feature of pauperism. Another is that the situation of pauperism has given such negative connotations to work that even work for the union is regarded with suspicion. Once the ethic of independence and self-respect through work has been destroyed, it is very difficult to replace it with any motivation to action. It has only been slowly that people have seen the value of working for each other, and discovered that their efforts can give each other more real support and assistance than can hostile dependence on the professional Social Services bureaucracies. Much of this help has been given informally. Already we have helped members who are homeless to be rehoused; we have organised and run our own children's parties for our members' kids; we have bought our own Union transport (a van which Jim converted into a mini-bus) which serves for everything from furniture removals to seaside outings. Very often the completely spontaneous Union activities—such as trips to the moors or the sea on fine days—are more popular than the more organised activities which have associations with work. But they are all examples of co-operation between claimants, and we will continue to find ways of helping each other which the authorities cannot stop, and which give us a better life without infringing our right to a basic income from claims.

We have developed these alternative systems partly because we have been excluded from the mainstream of society, but partly also because we can see what is wrong with that system. Society as a whole has sacrificed us for the sake of its material progress, and has denied us a fair share in its prosperity. It regards us as passive and useless paupers who have to be supported on state benefits. But from our position we can see the radical weakness of that society.

We no longer believe in its promises of a technological paradise. We see instead that an advanced economy still needs cheap raw materials, produced by cheap labour; still needs menials to do its dirty mopping-up jobs. We see that it uses up and pollutes the earth's resources more quickly than any previous society, and uses up and throws away redundant people at a far higher rate than before. We recognise how it destroys traditional patterns of family and social life and puts nothing in their place except individual greed and exploitation. We recognise that it concentrates wealth and power in fewer hands and widens the gap between rich and poor.

It may have taken exclusion from such a society to make us aware of the faults in it, but from the position of an outsider these become glaringly obvious. In many ways, these faults result from the submergence of old values which were once present, especially in working-class institutions. Thus our principles have often been old-fashioned ones, and represent a return to the values which underlay the first trade unions, friendly societies and co-operatives, attempting to rediscover the spirit of solidarity and collective co-operative action.

This has been necessary because of the truce that has been made between the present-day bureaucratic giants, which bear the names of working class institutions, and the big business class. It is necessary because, in agreeing to share a part of their wealth, they have come to share much of their competitive, individualistic ethos, and their greedy exploitation of the weak.

Our claimants' organisations may be poor by their standards, but they are richer in other ways. We are sustained by the values that they have forgotten; the willingness to work for others as well as ourselves, to give help without hope of reward, and to stand together in face of persecution. If we are to be excluded, to be set apart in a Bantustan of poverty, then these are the values that we will choose to live by. Although most people may prefer the alienated affluence of the technological kingdom of profit, we at least will be free, and in control of our own destinies. Our slogan will be 'Bantustan is Best'.

3 Implications

There has been plenty of evidence in recent years about what happens to societies in which there is a rigid division between Have and Have Not sectors, and members of these sectors are readily identifiable to each other. The most violent cases (involving these societies in a choice between repression or revolution) have occurred where the working class is divided on lines which are racial (as in South Africa) or religious (as in Northern Ireland) or geographical (as in East and West Pakistan).

In this country we are fortunate that no single one of these factors can be expected in the immediate future to mark off one sector of society from the rest, though there is a threat that race might do so before long. However, at this moment there is a deepening gulf developing between the sector represented by the worker who lives in a semi-detached house, earns £30 a week (including incentive bonuses) at his skilled trade, and pays rates and taxes; and the sector represented by the claimant, who earns £18 a week when he can get a job, and claims Family Income Supplement, rent rebates, free school meals and exemption from prescriptions charges. The worker may not attribute the claimant's actions, which he identifies as a drain on the nation's hard-pressed resources, to the fact that he is black or Catholic. He may at present just call him a scrounger or a layabout. But increasingly he will identify him as one of a class of such people which can be distinguished from his own class, whose members can be identified by behaviour which denotes inferiority.

In the past, the division between workers and claimants was fostered by the ruling class as a means of sustaining the work ethic. In a situation of full employment, and when work really did confer upon people a higher income and the status associated with independence, claimants could either be despised as workshy, or pitied as the poor. They were an example of what happened to those who were unwilling or unable to work, and thus they could be used to reinforce the will to work.

The situation under a Speenhamland System is not nearly so clear. Those whose earnings are below the prescribed level undermine the myth which sustained the work ethic. From the point of view of the working class (of those independent of state benefits) they are some form of inferior workers. From the point of view of the claiming class, they are claimants, forced into work.

The interests of the two classes thus are manifestly different. The worker tries to maximise his work (through overtime, bonuses, productivity incentive schemes etc.). He tries to minimise his contribution through rates and taxes. The claimant tries to maximise his income through claims, and to avoid work, which may often reduce his income, and which offers him no advantages. There is a real danger that this divergence of interests may result in a hardening of attitudes, so that two rigidly defined groups are formed, each antagonistic to the other. Even without the exacerbation of racial or religious differences, this division could become deep enough to produce organised conflict.

It is much easier for governments to create a Speenhamland situation than it is for them to undo it. The present rate of inflation ensures that the rates for supplementary benefits, and consequently the prescribed levels for Family Income Supplement, have to be raised regularly. Because the wages of the lowest paid are not rising as quickly, each 'concession' to the poor creates a larger claiming class and diminishes the working class. The process is accelerated by the present stagnation of the economy. The government is under pressure to increase consumption in order to give a boost to production and investment. To do this, it raises the levels of supplementary benefits, because the poor are more likely to spend all the extra money they get. This at once increases the claiming class by the number of workers whose wages were previously just above the old level. In holding the wages of the lowest paid down, and preferring a Speenhamland solution to the problem of the poverty this creates, governments are eating away the working class in their efforts to keep up the necessary level of consumption. In other words, rather than pay living wages to an independent workforce of those who make our products, our rulers prefer to increase the number of claimants whose work is forced labour; but they have to increase the allowances to these paupers to give them enough to buy the things they are making.

Once a man has taken the dive down into the claiming class, it requires a tremendous leap to get him back into the working class again. If he qualifies for Family Income Supplement, rent rebates, rate rebates, exemptions from prescription charges, free school meals and all the other selective benefits, there is no incentive for him to earn a few extra pounds just to lose all these benefits again. If he becomes unemployed, it will take a job with wages several pounds above the one he previously held to tempt him back into work of his own accord again. A family can join the claiming class at a stroke of a Whitehall pen, but nothing but a major increase in its earnings can put it back in the working class again. The proposed changes in the tax structure will do nothing to change this situation.

It would, therefore, require a very considerable effort by those who represent the working class to reintegrate its lost members who have joined the claiming class, to break down the division between workers and claimants, and to ensure that no man in work should have to depend on state subsidies for his existence. Only large-scale wage rises for low-paid workers could possibly bridge the gap. Only a deliberate policy, strenuously pursued, could produce a result which would require a reversal of the trend against the low-paid which has existed since productivity became the criterion for pay awards.

However, this is clearly not the intention of the established Labour movement. On the contrary, both the Trade Unions and the Labour Party are colluding with the split between the classes, or blindly advocating policies which can only widen the gulf between them. They are quite prepared to weep crocodile tears about the plight of the unemployed, the sick or pensioners. It is their policy to encourage the Conservative Government to raise levels of Social Security benefits and pensions. But their motivation for this is quite clear. They hope claimants will be grateful to them for representing their needs to the government. They ignore the fact that these same increases in the Social Security rates will diminish the class of independent workers and increase the number of paupers. Far from winning themselves support, they are creating the division which is building up the most dangerous source of opposition to their self-interested, greedy policies.

Far from seeking to close the gap between the pauper sector

P.—F

and independent workers, the Trade Unions and the Labour
Party are quite happy to see the Social Security system and the
various selective benefits (which the last government had begun
to initiate) used as a method of dealing with the problem of low
wages. They are quite content to see poverty side by side with
affluence as a social problem rather than a result of the economic
order they have helped to create. This is why members of the
claiming class, which has been brought into existence by their
policies, are coming to recognise the need to represent themselves through their own organisations and especially through
Claimants' Unions.

One of the greatest problems which face Claimants' Unions
as they try to establish themselves as an effective force, working on behalf of the claiming class, is their relations with the
established Labour movement, and with people in the working
class. Should they try to keep alive the remaining links between
claimants and workers, to seek to persuade the Trade Unions
and the Labour Party of their responsibilities towards the
pauper sector? Should they see the Labour Party and the Unions
as organisations which could be reformed, and to which they
should behave as constructive critics, as potential allies rather
than opponents?

The danger of this approach is that the activities of Claimants'
Unions could very easily be rendered safe and innocuous by
these much more powerful forces. The established Labour
movement would obviously prefer to see the Claimants' Union
as a sort of pressure group for higher social security benefits;
or as a kind of radical version of the Child Poverty Action
Group, making claimants more aware of their welfare rights,
and drawing the attention of the public to the plight of the poor.
This would simply serve their purpose of badgering the government to increase the levels of social security, which they are
interested in only for its expansionist effect on the economy as
a whole.

Claimants' Union have no intention of adopting this kind of
role. They are opposed in principle to the Social Security
system, its means tests, its humiliating claims procedure and its
authoritarian powers. Far from wishing to extend it, they want
it abolished. In so far as they are capable of acting together as
a pressure group, it would certainly not be of a reformist,

CPAG kind. They would tend to come together to press for some form of guaranteed income, a real living income, for people in work and out of it, that would not have to be crawled and grovelled for at the feet of a bureaucratic overlord.

However, in any case the structure of Claimants' Unions does not favour the function of a pressure group. There is only the loosest kind of federal structure, and there are no national officers. The antonomous local unions are the main units, and each of these has the power and the responsibility of making its own decisions about what line to take in the question of co-operation or conflict with local Labour Party and Trade Union interests.

In Newton Abbot we found initially that opportunities for working together with these groups seems to present themselves. There appeared to be occasions on which we could act as a pressure group for a particular change which our members would benefit from, and in which we could gain the support of the unions and the Labour Party. For instance, we campaigned for a direct labour building department of the local authority in order to relieve some of the unemployment in the building industry. This was in our early phase, when we were thinking mainly of our function in relation to the unemployed. We were perhaps not considering sufficiently the kind of wages that the local authority would have been prepared to pay, or the danger that some of our members could have been forced into low-paid jobs through our campaign. At any rate, we found that Labour councillors and the building Trade Unions were keen to co-operate with us and happy to see the initiative taken by an organisation which directly represented the unemployed, giving the campaign much more bite at a time when unemployment was becoming a political issue. In spite of considerable resistance by building employers and some conservative councillors, the pressure was eventually successful, and the council took the first steps towards the establishment of a direct works scheme.

However, this partial success has not led to closer co-operation. When we have attended meetings called by local Labour Parties and Trade Unions, what we have heard has mainly consisted of stale rhetoric and empty promises. The recuring theme has been the need for demonstrations against unemployment. Demonstrations give the impression of doing something about a problem without actually doing anything. People who spend the rest of the year in warm offices drawing good salaries take a day off to walk about in the streets, something that our members do every day of the year. They blame the present government for a situation largely created by the previous one. They make no mention of their policies or their productivity negotiations which are still making thousands redundant every week. They do not talk about providing decent income for every family or limiting the working week. If someone mentions lowering the retiring age they may nod their heads wisely, thus giving unthinking assent to the idea of condemning every worker to an extra five years of poverty, at the mercy of the Social Security system.

While we are happy to work with individuals from the Trade Unions and the Labour Party who recognise the realities of the situation they have helped to create, we have not been impressed with any great enthusiasm to initiate fields for common action between the Claimants' Union and the established Labour movement in our area. We realise that in many ways the Claimants' Union represents a very great threat to them. It threatens to expose their lack of real concern about the sector of the community that has been sacrificed by them, and to show up the hypocrisy that underlies so many of their official pronouncements.

The further threat that it represents is in making explicit the extent to which the unions and the Labour Party no longer represent the interest of ordinary workers in the long term. Some workers, particularly in those industries which are threatened with redundancies, are beginning to see the connection between the policies that have been adopted by union leaders and Labour politicians and their deteriorating working conditions, the insecurity of their jobs, and the queues of their former workmates at the Labour Exchanges. Claimants' Unions can give expression to the resentment felt by ordinary rank and file trade union members about the concentration of power in the hands of their national officials, about complicated productivity deals which are imposed upon them, and about the lack of concern about their opinions and needs involved in top-level national negotiations. Thus if Claimants' Unions cannot find an opportunity to co-operate with unions, they may well instead find themselves joining with workers at a local level, helping them to defy their union's national policies.

This is precisely what happened in Newton Abbot quite recently. The seventy workers at the power station were offered a £5 per week pay rise early last year as part of a national productivity deal which would have reduced the number of jobs at the station by twelve. They were promised that there would be no immediate redundancies, but that reductions in the workforce would eventually be made through early retirements and natural wastage. However, the men realised that, even if their own immediate prospects were not threatened by this productivity deal, the interests of twelve other unemployed people waiting for a vacancy in just such a job were very much at stake. They therefore decided to turn down the whole deal, and forego the pay-rise for the sake of protecting the jobs that would otherwise have disappeared, adding to the long-term unemployment problems of everyone in the area.

However, neither the management nor the union in the power industry were prepared to accept this isolated act of defiance, and a further campaign was launched to try to persuade the Newton Abbot workers to accept the productivity deal. Expensive management consultants were engaged by the Board to spend weeks interviewing the men to get them to change their minds. By December the matter was coming to a head again, but the power station workers found that on this occasion they were not without support. The Claimants' Union had been carrying out a leaflet campaign of its own against productivity deals, pointing out their causation of unemployment. Only a few weeks before the power station workers' decision was to be made, many such leaflets had been distributed at workplaces in the area, and they had all therefore had the opportunity of reading of the backing that we were giving them in their stand.

It was thus that a very surprised management consultant learnt from the workers when he outlined the productivity scheme to them that the Union was against it. When he assured them that their Union had fully endorsed the proposed deal he was again contradicted. When he asked what Union's statements they were refering to, he was told the Claimants' Union. At the decision, only three workers voted to accept the produc-

tivity deal, and the consultants returned to London, no doubt
wondering who on earth the Union which had so inconveniently
intervened might be.

There have been other instances of co-operation between
Claimants' Unions and workers and strikers in other areas. It
could well be that these are not isolated incidents, but indica-
tions of a movement among working people, who are increasingly aware of the disastrous consequences of their trade union
leaders' policies. The rising tide of unemployment and the
revulsion against the economic policies of governments of both
parties provided fertile ground in many factories for Claimants'
Unions' literature. The moral and intellectual bankruptcy of
the Labour Party establishment ensure that Claimants' Union
principles are refreshingly new and stimulating for people who
have suffered years of doubts and frustrations, and welcome the
opportunity of expressing themselves positively in resistance
against the pressures to betray their fellows, and in the long
run themselves, to which they have been subjected.

There are many militant trade unionists and political groups
who will be anxious to ensure that these links between Claimants
and workers are maintained and developed. These are the
people who believe that only a militant political struggle, re-
jecting the tepid reformism of the Labour Party and the unions
alike, can win anything worth having for the proletariat as a
whole. For such people—and a great number of active members of the Claimants' Unions would subscribe to this ideal—
only an increased economic and political awareness on the part
of all groups, the better paid, the worse paid and the unemployed, will achieve the sort of combined effort required to
redress the wrongs of the present situation.

There is a danger, however, that this aim of uniting
claimants and workers in active resistance, which already requires an organisational capability far greater than any which
now exists, will become harder rather than easier to achieve.
A succession of shocks, both political and industrial, have made
opinion among workers, especially the less secure and the lower
paid, much more susceptible to a militant ideology than it has
been in recent years. The defeat of the Labour government, the
Rolls Royce and the Upper Clyde crashes, the economic stagnation, unemployment and the miners' and dockers' strikes

have all contributed to this state of mind among workers, which has caused even the Labour Establishment to react with a marginal shift to the left. But it is doubtful whether this state of mind will survive the economic boom which will eventually be engineered by the Conservative government, and which will inevitably cause a drifting apart of those whose wages will benefit from the higher national output, and those whom the same economic circumstances will simply force into unacceptable employment. Such isolation will inevitably force the Claimants' Unions to think in terms of strategies which directly benefit their members, without reference to the interests of the non-claiming working class. It will strengthen the hand of those who are already arguing that claimants form a separate class which must pursue its own ends, and which can expect nothing from those who have been so conditioned by the industrial process that they have come to accept the capitalist's work ethic and to adopt his individualism and his personal greed.

The political implications of such a development might be considerable. In many ways, it would play right into the hands of the big business class. However small and insignificant the Claimants' Union movement might appear, if it can only continue to develop as it has done recently it will build itself into a force which could claim to give voice to the needs of a considerable sector of the population. To this extent it would express the very division which the ruling class has set out to create, and which would inevitably weaken any attempt at building a united political movement which might undermine the consensus politics of the business—labour truce. But, even more seriously in the short term, it would very probably give momentum to the growth of a working class following for the doctrines of Powellism. While a slump may provoke sympathy for the non-productive members of society, a boom would soon dissipate such feelings, and a militant claimants' movement would provoke a reaction from people who already resent having to 'work to keep layabouts like them'. The Tory Press and politicians would be quick to exploit such feelings and Claimants' Unions would rapidly find that they had lost the sympathy they briefly enjoyed.

This dilemma for Claimants' Unions is likely to be resolved, not by ideological disputations about whether or not claimants constitute a Marxian class, nor yet by short-term divisions about tactics, but by the long-term economic and political situation. There is a pauper sector already, and it is growing. All the economic trends are against it, and it is getting steadily poorer in relation to the rest of society. It is also increasingly more identifiable to itself and to others, as the government introduces more selective state benefits. Any movement which can begin to unite this class as a self-conscious interest goup which identifies its own needs and expresses them in conflict with other groups, will only be giving shape to an entity whose existence will already have been recognised by its members and by those outside it.

Britain must be the most class-conscious country in the world. In many ways the subtle slurs and stigmas of class take the place of cruder repressions and deprivations imposed on racial or religious grounds in other countries. But the distinction between workers and claimants is not simply a division of status related to the question of dependence on state benefits. It is a real question of economic interests, determined by the development of industrial technology and capitalist economic theory.

The fact is that technical sophistication and the logic of capitalist production have taken us to the point where workers increasingly cannot afford to buy the products they make out of their wages. But the level of production can only be maintained, and profits continue to be made, if these products are sold. Therefore, ways have to be found of making it possible for workers to consume more than their wages allow. The gigantic paraphernalia of hire purchase and credit has proved insufficient to maintain consumption in the face of the decline in purchasing power of the earnings of the lowest paid group. Thus the need to separate consumption from earnings through work is not a freakish feature of the present situation, but a direct result of expansionist philosophy which underlies Keynesian economic theory. Earnings have to be supplemented in order to allow the economy to grow.

Obviously, this result follows from a system in which the earnings of workers do not match the value of what they produce, and the mainstream of socialism has always been concerned with action directed to close this gap between wages and the value of worker's products. However, there is another way of attacking this system. The divorce between wages from work and income for consumption could be accepted, so long as income could be maximised, and work could be at a chosen limited level, and under the control of the worker. What is objectional about the Speenhamland system, after all, is not the notion of supplementing wages. It is the very low level of the supplement. It is the stigmatising method of providing it. And it is the enforced, slave labour which has to be undergone as a condition for qualification. If claimants as a class are to adopt the course of action which follows logically from their situation within the economic system, this would consist of (a) organised resistance to work on unfavourable terms (i.e. at wage rates lower than their *maximum* possible income from benefits and collective work when they are unemployed); (b) organised maximisation of income from claims; (c) the replacement of Social Security by a system which guarantees a regular income by right; (d) the organisation of schemes, under their own control, for deriving the fullest economic benefit from collective action consistent with their position as claimants— i.e. schemes for co-operative work, under their own control.

Such a programme of action should not be seen as contrary to the efforts of rank and file workers to improve their position. Actions aimed at securing higher basic wages for a shorter working week, coupled with bans on overtime and productivity dealing, are not only consistent with claimants' interests, but directly complementary to a claimants' programme. They combat wage slavery, and tend towards the establishment of a system in which the benefits of technological advance would be shared amongst a working class with a truly higher living standard. Above all, both could come together to fight for a guaranteed income that was not conditional upon forced labour.

However, the danger is that the adoption of such a programme would provoke very strong opposition, not only among the rulers, but also among right-wing workers. Claimants would be accused of living off the labour of workers, and of exploiting the generosity of the state. Bitterness and hatred directed at them might take organised form. Intimidation and violence might provoke a defensive reaction from claimants who in turn could organise for violent conflict. Already induced by their economic situation to live in a twilight zone on the edge of the law, because their situation places a premium on fraud, theft and illegal casual employment, claimants' organisations could easily take on the role of an illegal resistance movement.

In the long run, obviously, the hopes for any major change in our economic and political system must rest on the combined efforts of the whole proletariat, comprising workers and claimants. In the short run, however, there is good reason to suppose that if claimants wait for such a movement to come into existence, to organise its campaign and to carry it out, they will wait for ever. Such a movement is likely to start from the bottom, from claimants, and to be sustained by their efforts, in spite of persecution from governments and workers alike. Although in the nature of things they are least likely to be the beneficiaries of such a movement's eventual triumph, they are none the less probably required to make the greatest sacrifices and suffer the worst persecution to achieve this end.

Their position may be compared with that of the illegal and semi-legal working class organisational underground during the counter revolutionary years at the start of the Nineteenth Century. The Reform Act in 1832, which represented a triumphant gain in political and economic power for the middle class, was largely accomplished by pressure from working class organisations which threatened nothing less than revolution during this period. 'It had been the pecular feature of English development that, where we would expect to find a growing middle-class reform movement with a working-class tail, only later succeeded by an independent agitation of the working class, in fact the process was reversed ... The twenty-five years after 1795 may be seen as the years of the long counter-revolution, and in consequence the Radical movement remained largely working-class in character' (Thompson, op. cit., p. 888). In a similar way, the real resistance to the increasingly repressive system of our present political masters is likely to be based on the efforts of organisations of the claiming rather than the working class.

Just as in 1832 it was the middle class who exploited the immense popular unrest which expressed itself through working class organisations, and in the revolt of the rural paupers in 1830, so in some future years the organised Labour movement, which will no doubt condemn the resistance of claimants' organisations, may use a similar situation to their advantage. As the *Poor Man's Guardian* said in 1831: 'Threats of a "revolution" are employed by the middle classes and petty masters, but a violent revolution is not only beyond the means of those who threaten it, but is to them the greatest object of alarm; for they know that such a revolution can only be effected by the poor and despised millions, who, if excited to the step, might use it for their own advantage.' In a similar way, taxpaying ratepaying workers may use and betray the eventual culmination of the claimants' campaign for the right to be treated as human beings.

The process which gives rise to violent conflict as a prelude to such a culmination is one which is dolefully familiar from recent history in other countries. The ruling class is engaged in an intricate juggling act, by which it is keeping down wages, keeping up the consumer income of the claimant, and playing off the working class against the claiming class. Like all conservative paternalists, they tend to underestimate the prejudice and hatred they engender between those they patronisingly condemn to second-class dependency and those they divide off into their own fold, to feed with the crumbs of a privileged status. Conservatives tend always to believe that dependants are basically grateful to exist on their charity. They also tend to believe that their supporters share their feelings of indulgent paternalism towards them. When, therefore, there arise the first stirrings of a movement for resistance among the dependent class, they mistakenly make some concessions to it, treating the participants as a kindly master might a difficult servant. They are then caught up in the backlash of their supporters, furious that the master's favours have been bestowed upon the inferior and unworthy. In the confrontation that this provokes, they inevitably but inconsistently side with their protégés against the new movement and thus bring down on their heads greater hatred than existed before.

There has been a recent example of this sort of process in the concession over earnings by unemployed people. At the Budget, this was raised from $33\frac{1}{2}$ pence to 75 pence per day. It would be interesting to know what lay behind this concession; we in the Newton Abbot Claimants' Union would like to believe it had some relation to our campaign, in which we had stressed the harshness of the regulations. However, this concession will not appease us in any way. On the contrary it will make it possible for us openly and straightforwardly to organise the scheme which hitherto we have had to conduct by devious processes. Our work scheme can, in October, be set up under an arrangement which will legitimately allow our members to work for up to £4.50 per week without losing benefits. If we can get a substantial number of our members working for this extra money, we will have created a situation in which it is very much more in their interests to avoid being forced back into badly-paid regular employment. We will be able to make it plain that we are trying to organise resistance to the kind of slave labour that our members have had imposed upon them. This will make us much more unpopular, but it will take us forward in our struggle to win a better standard of living for the claiming class.

Only a ruthless regime will repress the first glimmer of resistance from its oppressed sector. Those with liberal consciences to appease make concessions in the hope of buying off the new militants. Such concessions are far more dangerous to themselves. They arouse expectations which are inevitably disappointed in what follows. The ruling class has no intention of granting justice or equality to its paupers. It is simply bribing them to be more passive and dependent. Thus it is surprised and angry when they are not satisfied with larger doles, or some spurious representation. The ruling class cannot imagine that paupers should want to escape from their happy state of dependency. Too late they try to clamp down on the drive to freedom that they have inadvertently stimulated.

Once a situation has been created in which a group identifies itself as excluded from any benefits of taking part in a system which bestows some advantages on others, there are no reforms or concessions that can be effectively made to such a group short of total reintegration into the system as a whole. For a group or class with the status of second-class citizens, being better off second class citizens merely makes it easier to organise resistance. For a group or class who have realised that they have different interests from the rest of the community, concessions will simply enable them to pursue these interests more effectively. If it is in the interests of paupers to resist forced work, to maximise claims and to use their energies to organise co-operative self-help projects, they will only turn concessions to their advantage in carrying out these activities. They will not become less militant and less conscious of their status and interests as claimants, once this consciousness has been gained. Only the kind of total reorganisation of the wage structure required to make paupers' interests coincide with workers' again would achieve the aim of reintegrating their attitudes towards work with those which prevail in the rest of the community.

Such a huge restructuring is unlikely to occur under our present system. The likelihood, therefore, is that claimants will be forced to take action in pursuit of their interests which will increasingly alienate not only the rulers but also a section of the working class. Claimants and their organisations will be seen as suitable objects for persecution not only by the authorities, but also by right-wing working-class groups, who, in their own areas, may well take the law into their own hands in the matter of intimidating and suppressing claimants' resistance. Not only will the individualistic assertions of paupers' frustrations with their slavish status—theft, fraud, violence and (in country areas, still linking the last Speenhamland era with present) poaching—continued to increase and to be harshly punished; but organised efforts to combat the degradation of their position will be equally firmly suppressed.

Those who feel secure in the belief that violence is not part of our political (or even our criminal) tradition should recall that our present standards are of relatively recent origin. Revolution and a wave of violent crime accompanied our last Speenhamland period. Any system which divides the working class and creates economic justifications for prejudice and resentment between the two groups is virtually guaranteeing for itself a violent episode. It is true that at the present time the division between the two groups is not yet rigid or clear cut. Many people alternate between pauperism and independence; for many poverty is a short-term feature of life, associated with the age of their children, an illness, an accident or an economic recession. For others, however, it is becoming a permanent feature of life, associated with low earning power, slum housing, disablement, chronic sickness, poor employment prospects or old age. Government policies ensure that the status of such people—through inflation and the introduction of fresh selective benefits—will become more distinguished from that of members of the independent working class. It is among such people, in their ghettoes, that an increasingly militant paupers' ideology will arise, and will express itself in spite of persecution, through its own organisations.

At present Claimants' Unions, as the first of such organisations, are still engaged in activities which are unobjectionable by almost any standards. The vast majority of members' daily transactions with each other consist in simple acts of human kindness between individuals. Members help each other to be aware of their rights; lend each other a hand in difficult situations; relieve distress with sympathy and practical help. The Union's function could be seen simply as helping people with the kind of crises that they might otherwise have found support in dealing with through memberships of trade unions, friendly societies or any form of voluntary organisation, had not their status as claimants virtually excluded them from membership of any such organisations. The dictates of ordinary human compassion demand that a self-help group like a Claimants' Union should exist to provide some comfort and relief by claimants for claimants. But this cannot be the eventual function of the unions. For as claimants become more aware of their situation, they will use their links with each other to further their interests, as these are determined by the economic system. Already the literature of the Claimants' Union Movement reflects a very full awareness of this situation, and of its implications for them.

The only strength in the paupers' present position lies in their role as consumers, where at present they are needed to bolster up flagging demand on the home market. But even this economic advantage may prove temporary. Generosity to claimants at a time of recession is not likely to survive a boom. At the present time the pauper sector is in the position of a discarded colony. Although it is no longer so necessary as a source of cheap labour to produce raw materials, it is still valuable as a market for surplus products. However, unlike a discarded colony, this sector can be reclaimed as cut-price man-power when boom conditions return, and then it is likely to feel the force both of the drive to get claimants back into work, and of any restrictions on spending which may become necessary if the economy becomes over-heated.

It would be easy for good liberal middle-class people to deceive themselves that Claimants' Unions represent no more than welfare-orientated self-help groups for the poor. Such people would no doubt like to support Claimants' Unions as manifestations of a desire for independence and self-respect among recipients of social security, or as rather more militant welfare-rights groups. The social and political significance of Claimants' Unions is far deeper that this. They indicate that the lot of the pauper sector at the bottom of society is growing worse, and that this sector, divided off from the rest, having lost all control over the rest of its existence, is seeking to control the only thing left to it, its access to state benefits.

Even this last remaining piece of life is becoming more anonymous and depersonalised, more frustrating and soul-destroying for paupers. Social Security offices are being rapidly centralised, so that enormous, impersonal blocks are replacing the old-style neighbourhood offices. Claimants are being herded together like animals in these temples of bureaucratic formalism. The posters which encourage them to believe they have rights to benefits are systematically denied by the processes which make access to such benefits more difficult—through the geographical and social remoteness of the offices. New systems are being adopted which make claiming more impersonal. There are to be fewer visiting officers, and more forms sent through the post to be filled in. The Social Security system is ceasing to be represented by a familiar local officer, who is being replaced by all the symbols of anonymous, centralised authority.

The complexities of new selective benefits occupy an increasing amount of the claimant's time and energies. Being a pauper is developing into a full-time job. With this comes the claims mentality—an attitude of mind in which all else is secondary to the question of how to get more from Social Security, and all the frustration and resentment generated by this degraded existence is directed against this one institution. What might be described as militant dependency—which is characteristic of most Claimants' Union literature—is a direct result of the kind of system that has been adopted for creating and managing pauperism.

This is why the Newton Abbot Claimants' Union, which has

tried to combine an effective claims function with more outward-looking self-help projects, is likely to become less typical of the movement as a whole, and ultimately less viable in itself. Already at the time of writing it is chiefly preoccupied with a battle to resist plans to close down the local Social Security office in Newton Abbot, and to transfer all its claimants to Torquay. This move would not only cause considerable hardship to those with urgent needs in Newton Abbot, it would also inevitably lead to a change of policy and emphasis within the Union. As claims work became more time-consuming and difficult, more manpower and energy would be required for this, as is already happening over the organisation of the protest campaign. The problems of getting a basic income from the Department may exclude all other projects, and ultimately our self-help schemes, which originally appeared to be an impudent challenge to the system, may be nostalgically recalled as last manifestations of independence and moderation.

The struggle which faces the paupers in our society is an arduous one. All the power and the resources are on the side of their opponents. There is very little room for compromise between the two sides, and the very desperation of the paupers' position makes it all the more likely that in the long run they will be forced to adopt tactics which are very much more militant than those which they employ today.

At present, Claimants' Unions are seeking proper recognition as representatives of the claiming class. They are demanding the right for claimants to have an adequate income without resorting to the degrading procedures of the Social Security bureaucracy. They are demanding that claimants should have more control over the departments which are supposed to serve them. These demands constitute no more than a programme for co-existence with a limited degree of freedom for the pauper sector of economy. In the long run, the needs of paupers are likely to be expressed more forcefully, both in the political arena and in the streets.